AF241307

The ORACLE

A modern day success story
that you'd be crazy not to
make your own

Lachlan Cameron

To an old friend Simon Bernard,
whose untimely death taught me the importance
of planning as though you will live forever
but living as though you could die today.

To my beloved Matilda and Jack,
within these pages is the secret to living
a remarkable life – should you ever need it.

First published in 2021 by Lachlan Cameron

© Lachlan Cameron 2021

The moral rights of the author have been asserted

All rights reserved. Except as permitted under the *Australian Copyright Act 1968*
(for example, a fair dealing for the purposes of study, research, criticism or review), no part
of this book may be reproduced, stored in a retrieval system, communicated or transmitted
in any form or by any means without prior written permission.

All inquiries should be made to the author.

A catalogue entry for this book is available from the National Library of Australia.

ISBN: 978-1-922553-26-3

Cover design by Andrew Brown
Printed in Australia by McPherson's Printing
Project management and text design by Publish Central

The paper this book is printed on is certified as environmentally friendly.

Disclaimer: The material in this publication is of the nature of general comment only, and
does not represent professional advice. It is not intended to provide specific guidance for
particular circumstances and it should not be relied on as the basis for any decision to take
action or not take action on any matter which it covers. Readers should obtain professional
advice where appropriate, before making any such decision. To the maximum extent
permitted by law, the author and publisher disclaim all responsibility and liability to any
person, arising directly or indirectly from any person taking or not taking action based on
the information in this publication.

CONTENTS

Introduction

This story begins when a chance meeting with a fortuneteller was to change my life forever. Yet, this is not a story about chance: this is a story about *choice*.

I was a young man just beginning that journey we call life, and she was a mystic, with a skill beyond my reckoning. I was about to have my future told, and what I learnt would fundamentally alter my understanding of life.

Two possible futures

What I hadn't appreciated at the time – and, I suspect, many of you still don't – is that we all have *two* possible futures, not one. That seemingly small revelation was to change my life forever, and if you fully appreciate what I just said, it will change yours too.

The first future that she predicted was what you might call an *ordinary* life. The type of life experienced by the vast majority of people. A little love, a little success, a little wealth, and a rather fleeting sense of achievement and happiness. In many ways a decent life, but somehow, one only half-lived. A life weighed down by doubt and a sense of missed opportunity, of unfilled potential, and a sense that – somehow – I was not quite good enough and did not have quite enough to be truly happy.

Fortunately, the second future was far more promising. It was a life marked by a profusion of wealth, great health, remarkable achievements, abundant love and most important of all, significant and enduring happiness – what you would call a *remarkable* life.

'So, which will it be?' I asked, frustrated at the prospect of two decidedly different outcomes.

'That I cannot tell,' she said.

My next question was an obvious one: 'But what do I need to do to live one life versus the other? A *remarkable* life versus an *ordinary* life?'

In many ways her response has driven me ever since.

'I really don't know,' she said. 'You'll have to work that out for yourself.'

So that's what I did. Or, more correctly, that's what I'm *doing*.

While I still have much to learn, I have made it my business to discover what it takes to live a *remarkable* life. To discover the principles, used by only a handful of the population at any point in time, to ensure good fortune, luck and opportunity. Those principles used to secure wealth, health and happiness.

Applying what I learnt enabled me to go on to live a *remarkable* life. I met and fell in love with an extraordinary woman, raised two wonderful children and educated them in the finest schools. We have traveled the world, lived in a number of truly amazing places, and gathered around us a small group of incredible friends. I have had the opportunity to open and grow new businesses around the globe, and provide for myself and my family all that we could possibly desire. In short, I secured my health, wealth and happiness.

I tell you this not to impress you, but to impress upon you just how rich and rewarding life can be. While there is still much for me to understand, I desperately want to share with you what I have already learnt – before it is too late – so you, too, can live a *remarkable* life.

My task has been to travel time, uncover the pattern of success, test it, trial it, and turn it into a reliable system that you can apply to your own life. As I have satisfied the vast majority of my own desires, my interest now turns increasingly to helping others. The system this book is about to unveil will be my legacy.

A holistic blueprint

Although much of what you'll learn here isn't new, the system that brings it all together is. While the work of others in this space is admirable, their tendency to focus narrowly on a singular theme – as the secret to success – will not deliver true and lasting success. To achieve that, you need a far more holistic blueprint. That is what we will create here together.

Like a great chef, The Oracle will guide you in collecting the right ingredients in the right quantities and then explain how to combine those ingredients with the correct amount of energy to create the desired outcome – a truly *remarkable* life.

As you can imagine, this is complex to work out in the first place, but very simple to replicate once you have the recipe. With recipe in hand, you simply need to follow the steps.

But you won't be on your own. The Oracle is here to act as your guide – a role he genuinely relishes and is rather excited to perform. Of course, he gets to do all the talking while you undertake all the work, but I feel comfortable with that exchange. Not because we are lazy but because I know you need some help, and I feel comfortable that we can provide real and lasting value. Value worth far more than the cost of this book.

Sound appealing? I suspect the answer to that is *yes*. So, what's the catch? Well, the problem is that it's not going to be easy. Simple, yes – but easy, no. That's the catch. So, let's deal with that elephant now.

You're going to have to work hard at this before you get it right. That's not to say it's not eminently doable, because it is. But you will have to change quite a few things about the way you think and what you do. And change is never easy. Whenever you see a successful person, you only see the public victories, never the hard work it took to reach that point.

The good news, however, is that life is much simpler than you thought. There are only five things that really matter, and you can be highly successful in each once you know how.

What you are about to discover will place you so far ahead of the pack you'll wonder why, with all those years of education, you weren't taught this sooner. You'll wonder why you learned all that other stuff but not this.

You see, the life we live, like most systems, is very sensitive to the starting conditions. A tiny difference in the 'push' you receive at the beginning will cause a big difference to where you end up. This book is designed to give you the ultimate *push*, and that *push* will change everything.

A dependable, repeatable process

At the outset, what you need to appreciate is that *people don't fail*, it's the system they are using that fails them. Success is not the byproduct of chance but rather the outcome of a system. Within these pages you will find *the system*. A dependable, repeatable process capable of delivering *remarkable* success – laid bare for all to see.

In the end, all you require will be distilled into a simple *Personal Life Plan*. A straightforward document that you can review in less than 10 minutes a day, yet its unique and profound insights will change your life forever.

You have two possible futures, not one. It's now The Oracle's job to prevent you from settling for an *ordinary* life while you could still achieve a *remarkable* one.

Good luck and enjoy the journey.

Lachlan

Part One

THE PROBLEM

TIME IS RUNNING OUT

'No frickin' way – you can't be serious?' was all I could muster as I sunk back into my chair staring at the piece of paper before me.

A few minutes earlier the person I generally considered to be my best friend had taken great delight in showing me our lives in months ... and it wasn't pretty.

On the sheet she'd placed in front of me was a series of small squares – each representing a month of life – from birth to age 93.

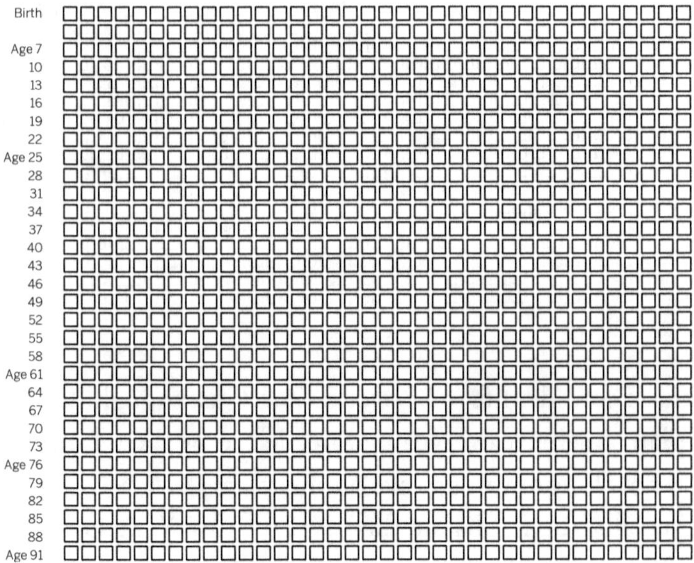

'So, that's all there is! Can you believe it?' she said with genuine enthusiasm. 'At best, we've only got this many months in our entire life! Isn't that crazy?'

I could tell she found the realization that there were surprisingly few months at our disposal to be truly liberating.

I wasn't feeling it.

I had seen versions of this previously but never really stopped to fully appreciate its ramifications. Now things were different. She had me place an 'X' on the box that reflected my current age – 26 – and a second one on a number I considered to be 'old'.

I found myself choosing 65.

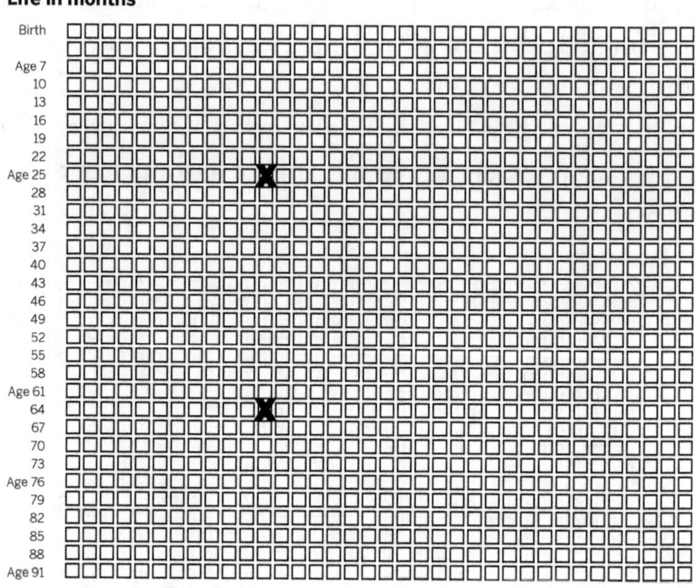

Not that I consider life to be over at 65 – I just thought I should at least plan to achieve everything I needed to by then. I mean, who knows how long any of us have on this planet?

After all, Tupac Shakur died at 25, Amy Winehouse at 27, Paul Walker at 40, Bon Scott at 33 and The Notorious B.I.G. at 24. Then there was John Lennon at 40, Mozart at 35, Alexander the Great at 32, Jimi Hendrix at 27, while Bob Marley, Marilyn Monroe and Princess Diana all died at 36. Of course, I could go on, but I won't.

Up until that moment life had always seemed so bountiful, with plenty of time to do what I wanted. It now dawned on me, with a rising sense of nausea, that I may be leaving things too late.

If I covered up the months that had already passed, and the ones at the end that I didn't want to rely on, then there weren't many left; not nearly as many as I had expected there to be. A horrendously small number, in fact.

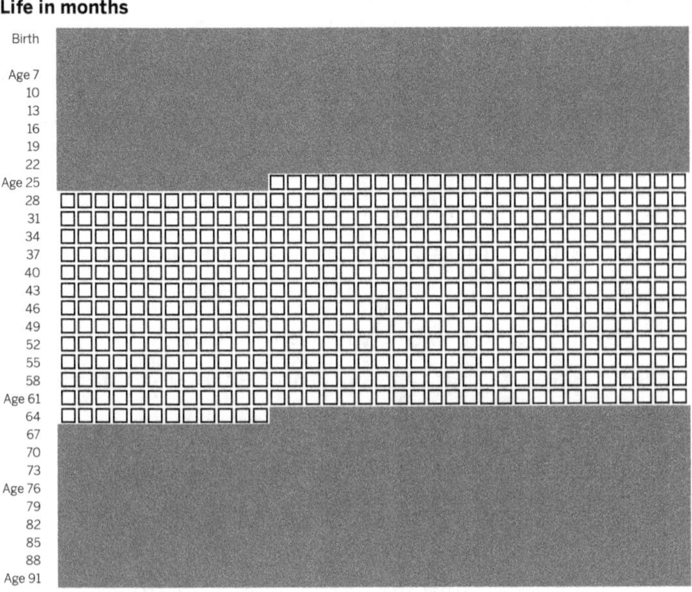

And what did I have to show for the time that had already passed? *Very little*, I thought rather self-consciously. Sure, I had a decent job, a few good friends and was in a nice relationship, but I hadn't achieved anything of real note. I hadn't really left my mark. I hadn't really made a difference. Yet, as silly as it may sound, I could sense a huge unrealized potential in me, the potential to be great, the ability to make a difference.

As I stared at the tiny squares, it was obvious that if I wanted my life to be meaningful, purposeful and extraordinary – and I did – and if I wanted to leave my mark on the world – and I did – then I needed to get going because there wasn't a lot of time to spare.

That was four days ago ...

Are we all destined for ordinary?

Since then, in an attempt to ease my anxious mind, having witnessed the distress our last interaction had caused me, the same friend made matters even worse. She lent me her favorite book on Buddhism, claiming that within its pages I would find peace. Yet its effect was the exact opposite.

I mean, call me a cynic if you want, but having sat under the Bodhi Tree for goodness knows how many days, Buddha's great realization appeared to be that we humans are *not* naturally inclined to live a remarkable life. That our natural state is one of suffering, misery, dissatisfaction and a rather fleeting sense of happiness – what you and I would call an *ordinary* life at best.

How was I expected to find any consolation in that?

It would appear that we are inherently dysfunctional and operate under a veil of delusion. In Hinduism it is called 'maya', in Buddhism it is called 'dukkha', and the Christians refer to it as 'original sin' – which, when properly translated, means 'missing the point of existence'.

And, if I looked around me, it was hard to dispute.

We certainly did appear to be missing the point of existence. The planet has never been more toxic, and I was part of the most in-debt, obese, addicted and medicated adult cohort in history. Part of a society that was being torn apart by inequality, fear, greed and a delusional sense of self; a society that had murdered more than 100 million of its citizens in the 20th century alone.

How ridiculous is that? I mean, it's really quite hard to fathom that we could regard this as anything but madness.

In stark contrast to this, I wanted to live a remarkable life – a life marked by great health, freedom, remarkable achievements, abundant love and enduring happiness. I wanted to make the world a better place for myself, and others.

But, and this was a big but, if our natural inclination and way of approaching life meant we would *not* typically live a remarkable life and happiness would remain an elusive desire, what was I to do?

Fortunately, all was not lost. Buddha did go on to offer us hope, essentially declaring that you can live a remarkable life *once you know how*.

That's right – despite his dire proclamation that we humans are *not* naturally inclined to live a remarkable life, he agreed that a complete cure was in fact available.

Well, at least there was hope. What had become increasingly evident, however, was just how rare living that *remarkable* life was. Exceedingly rare, in fact.

Nevertheless, there were those who had done it and those who were doing it, which meant, at least in theory, that it was also available to me. It wasn't going to be easy, however. This much I knew. I would most definitely need some help.

But from where?

FINDING HELP

When challenged, it has been said that we humans tend to respond in one of two ways: fight or flight. I chose *flight*, and headed down to Yellowstones, one of the local poolhalls, where I had every intention of using cheap liquor, merriment and a few rounds of pool to at least temporarily numb my growing unease.

It soon became evident that I wasn't alone in my thinking either. The place was packed. A heaving mass of young adults, having fun, escaping the realities of everyday life.

As the evening revelries escalated, my worries dissipated, my head now awash with alcohol, music, talking and laughter. A welcome relief from confronting the challenges of an unremarkable life.

Seeking a momentary reprieve from the festivities, I perched in a quiet corner at the edge of the room, preparing myself for another onslaught.

'Looks like you're in for a big night,' came the comment over my right shoulder. Startled, I swung around, assuming quite wrongly that I had been alone, only to find a rather composed man seated almost upon me. I now wondered why I hadn't noticed him earlier as he certainly stuck out from the crowd.

His T-shirt hung loosely from his lean frame. His face bore a fine dark stubble over tanned skin that indicated plenty of time spent outdoors. It was hard to guess his age; while aspects of his complexion suggested he was young, the hard-fought furrows around his forehead implied he was more likely to be middle-aged. Although his manner appeared relaxed and casual, there was an unexpected alertness radiating outward. This was totally at odds among the intoxicated crowd that filled the room.

'You might be a bit disappointed if you're looking to get lucky here tonight,' I said jokingly, alluding to his mismatch with those in the room.

'I'm already lucky, so just looking,' he responded with a smile.

'Looking for what?' I asked, bemused by his response.

'Exactly,' he responded.

'What type of answer is that?' I said a little more abruptly than I had intended, surprising myself in the process. I softened my demeanor to make amends, and attempted a reassuring smile.

'Well, for me this is perfect research. You and your friends here,' he said, waving his arm across the space, 'are my target market, and whenever I'm in a new city I like to spend some time at the city's favorite hangouts to understand the locals a little better. The concierge at my hotel suggested I come here.'

I now picked up on the fact that he had an accent, and this – combined with his reference to a hotel – confirmed that he was from out of town, although from where I could not tell.

'So, what brings *you* here tonight?' he now asked me, interrupting my train of thought.

'Well ... I suppose I'm drowning my sorrows like everyone else,' I said, gesturing towards the crowd and spilling half the contents of my glass in the process. 'Oops,' I said. 'Sorry about that. I may have had a little too much to drink.'

I then unexpectedly found myself explaining the lead up to tonight. How it had suddenly dawned on me how little time I had left to make my mark on the world, how my life was okay, but how little I had really achieved to date, how the odds were actually against me achieving the life I wanted so instead I was likely to end up living this rather ordinary life unless I did things radically differently, but just what things I needed to do differently I didn't know! Yet I felt this huge unrealized potential in me, the potential to be great ... on and on I went.

I wouldn't normally have been so forthcoming with a stranger but there was something in his manner that encouraged confession, and as I talked, I found a surprising calm washed over me. Before long I realized I was now breathing deeply and rhythmically as I spoke. The whole experience was quite euphoric. I stopped abruptly mid-sentence ...

'How'd you do that?' I said, facing my new neighbor, intrigued.

He looked at me with a perceptive smile. 'Just a party trick I picked up along the way.'

'Wow, if you bottled that you could make a lot of money.'

'You think so?' he said with a knowing smirk that made me sit up and take greater interest.

Who are you?

'Who are you?' I said, my curiosity now seriously triggered.

'Well ... that is a question I always find hard to answer,' he responded. 'Just like you, I am the spirit that fills the interspaces of the universe, but I suspect that's not what you had in mind with your question. Is it? If you are asking me what I do, then I am an architect.'

'Cool,' I said. 'I always wanted to be an architect, and then I spoke to an old family friend who had been an architect for many years and he said if I wanted to design buildings I should become a property developer instead. So that's what I did, or more accurately that's what I'm doing, property development, and so far, it's been really enjoyable.'

I realized that once again, I was now babbling a little more than I should, so I attempted to turn the conversation back to my mysterious neighbor.

'Do you design houses?' I asked.

'No, I design people's lives.'

'Oh, I see. Well, that's not what I expected. I didn't know people did that.'

'Well, you're right, there's not many of us that do, but there seems to be plenty of demand.'

'Hell, I can see why. I could certainly do with a bit of that.'

In response he reached inside his trouser pocket and pulled out a piece of folded white paper and handed it to me. 'Well, maybe I could help you,' he said.

'What's this?' I asked, and began to unfold it with intrigue. The man certainly had a captivating mystique, so I was fascinated to see what was next.

The sheet turned out to be a small promotional flyer, which I found myself reading slowly – as you do when you've had too much to drink.

THE ORACLE

All the way from Australia

One of the world's foremost authorities on

How to Live Your Life.

A sage of divine wisdom with a surprisingly fresh perspective on living the good life.

Why work out the rules for yourself?

Life's big questions have already been answered.

Join us this Friday @ 7pm

Location: Seattle Community Library

'Who's The Oracle?' I asked, turning back to my companion, but I was abruptly sidetracked when a guy, who had clearly had far too much to drink, bumped into me, emptying the contents of his glass in my lap.

'Hey, careful there,' I protested, as I shot out of my seat to wipe myself clean. 'Oh bugger, it's got all over your piece of paper,' I said with concern, wiping it down as best I could. 'I hope you have more of these?' I asked, turning, ready to plead my innocence ... but he was gone!

'What the heck?' I said quietly. *Where did he go?*

I looked around the room but could not see any trace of him. *Well that's weird,* I thought to myself. I hoped I wasn't imagining it, but realized the sheet of paper I was holding was far from imaginary.

Well, maybe this could be the help I am looking for, I thought to myself. Maybe I *had* found the answer in a poolhall, though not as I'd expected.

'Here's to fate,' I said with a cheer, toasting the room: 7pm Friday at the community library. I will most definitely be there!

With that, I emptied the remaining contents of my glass in a single swallow and plunged back into the evening's fun.

THE ORACLE

As I found a place to sit among the gathering crowd, I was surprised by the modest number of attendees.

If this person did indeed have all the answers, then surely he would attract a much larger crowd? Maybe being here was a mistake? Maybe this wasn't going to be so enlightening after all?

I now wondered whether I should leave while I still had a chance. As my doubts grew and I started to rise from my seat, a door to the side of the room opened and in walked the mysterious stranger from the poolhall.

Once again, he was dressed rather casually, but befitting of the manner in which he now moved across the room: an act he performed with great ease, more in keeping with an unencumbered child than a middle-aged man. He carried with him a definite air of excitement and anticipation – mine or his I could not tell.

Most of all, what struck me was his apparent contradiction. How could he simultaneously radiate an acute alertness and yet at the same time a deep, profound calm? *How is that possible?* I wondered. He took his seat on an elevated stool at the front of the room, while I edged back into mine.

Looking back now, leaving would have been a big mistake.

You need to see yourself and the world in a new light

'Welcome,' he said, acknowledging the crowd in front of him. 'I see you and bring you into being.' After an extended pause in which he actually appeared to be doing just that – taking us all into his being – he continued.

'You need to see yourself and the world in a new light.

'The limits you place on yourself and the assumptions you make about who you are and what you are capable of are nonsense. We are not what anybody tells us. Our perceived limitations are not real.

'You have no idea who you really are and what you are really capable of,' he exclaimed.

'We,' he said, placing particular emphasis on the word *we* and extending his arms to encompass the entire room, 'do not understand what we are really capable of!

'You are the key to saving the world. How could you be anything less?

'Yet, you have unintentionally created a prison for yourself – a self-imposed, self-limiting construct that excludes you from an endless array of possibilities and separates you from your true nature. This is the worst kind of prison – the one we build for ourselves. So, it's time for you to break free, and it's my job to help you do that. The goal is freedom, and the key is in your pocket.'

I do like the sound of that, I thought to myself. *That's exactly what I wanted to hear.* I could sense there was so much more potential inside me and I desperately wanted to set it free.

'Now, my friends,' he said, engulfing us in a warm smile, 'this is something I am very excited to be part of, so I thank you for the opportunity.

'You are wise to be getting some guidance,' he added. 'I say that because many of the most important things you need to understand about the world are neither intuitive nor obvious. Which means, you are unlikely to discover them for yourself for some time, if at all.'

I pondered that thought and knew he was right. Life is more complicated than we think, and it makes sense to get some help.

'Like the man who jumps out of a ninetieth-floor window on a bet and says to himself as he passes the tenth floor, *so far so good*, far too many of you are getting life terribly wrong but don't realize it yet. My fear is that by the time you do, it will be too late.'

His analogy drew a few nervous chuckles from the crowd. I myself reflected that his observation was likely to be disturbingly close to the truth as far as my own life was concerned. My thoughts returned to the 'life in months' diagram, and how rapidly I was churning through the time I had available, and how on my current trajectory I was likely to reach the end before I had really begun.

'Have you ever heard the expression, "dead too soon and wise too late"?' he asked.

'Well, I don't want any of you to fall victim to that. I don't want any of you to miss the opportunity to be fabulous and to live a remarkable, as opposed to an *ordinary*, life. That's why I am here tonight. And rest assured, any ordinary person can live a remarkable life ... once they know how.'

He now had my full attention – any remaining doubts had faded – and I was happy that I had come. I could sense that here before me was a person of great ability and wisdom. I looked at the faces around me to see how others were reacting. I suspect they felt the same, as all eyes were focused on The Oracle.

'You have the ability to leave here at the end of our time together a very different person to the one who just heard me utter that sentence. That's the miraculous thing about the human condition; you are totally reprogrammable.

'And programmed you are!' he said with discernible passion. 'Have no doubt about that. Round one occurred in your mother's womb to prepare you for the outside world. It was there that you established an initial behavioral program based on your mother's perception of the world.

'Then from birth to around age seven, your *round two* programming followed. Here you took on board a multitude of additional information from everyday life. In theory, all the remaining information you needed to survive, informed by your early experiences and, in the most part, others' views of you.

'Your parents call you shy. Your grandparents tell you to mind your place. Your siblings refer to you as clumsy. Your teachers tell you not to get ahead of yourself. Your friends call you an idiot. You consider yourself good at some things and not at others.

'And that's where the programming ends for most of us. In most cases we are just frightened and confused seven-year-old children trapped in an adult's body.'

There was a mix of laughter and some awkward shifting in seats.

'I like the fact you're laughing at this prospect,' The Oracle contended, 'but I also hope you appreciate that you have some serious work to do. Unless you take the time to reprogram yourself as a young adult, the program that you will continue running, the program that now determines your view of yourself and the world, has been cobbled together by a confused seven-year-old child. Full of destructive and limiting beliefs that are unlikely to support your current dreams and wishes.

'Round one was all about your mother's view of the world. Round two was all about what others think of you – or more precisely, what you think others think of you – because most of the time we have no idea what they are really thinking.

'Regardless, none of it is yours. It's as though you are acting in someone else's play. You have lost connection with your true nature.'

He got up from his chair, moved to the whiteboard and drew a large circle, which was divided into four segments, in between which he wrote the words: Embryo, Child, Adult and Sage.

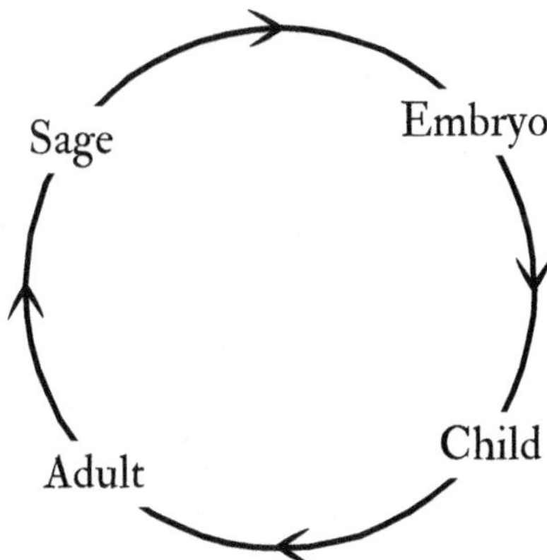

'In most cases, you are here,' said The Oracle, pointing to the word Child, 'and you need to move at least to here,' he said, pointing to the word Adult, 'and ideally to here.' He was now pointing to the word Sage.

'But I'm already an adult, you think to yourself! What's this guy on about?

'Well, physically yes, you are. I have no doubt that's the case – you drink, make love and grow hair where it's not wanted, but emotionally most people are stuck here,' he said, pointing again to the word Child.

Where was I, I wondered? I suspected there was plenty of that frightened and confused seven-year-old child still lurking about. I would like to think that I am an adult, but now I wondered. Although I would never have admitted that previously.

'But don't despair,' added The Oracle in welcome encouragement, as if sensing our uncertainty. 'We can get you to where you need to go, if you are prepared to undo a lot of that round one and two programming.

'To do that, however, you will need to undertake a new *round three* reprogramming process, and can I say that is likely to be the most important thing you will ever do.

'Seriously!' said The Oracle, emphasizing his point, 'I cannot imagine anything more important. It's time for you to evolve.

It's time to stop, reflect and recalibrate yourself. Work out who you really are, what you really stand for and what you really want to be. It's time to write your own story. Author your own life.'

I was inspired by that thought. I certainly loved the idea of authoring my own life.

'You can reinvent yourself from this point forth. Never doubt that for a moment! Each day is an opportunity for a new and better version of what existed yesterday. And, while there is no point in proving your superiority over others, there is a lot to be gained in proving your superiority over your former self.

'Although you may not be able to change others, you can and must change *yourself*. After all, if you are not growing – being the biological creature that you are – then technically you are dead.'

This comment attracted laughter from the room.

'Ah good, signs of biological life,' said The Oracle, lightening the mood.

Growth is an important aspect of achieving your full potential

'I know some of you may feel that there is too much focus on growth in the world, but the energy of nature is always moving towards growth and creation, and we as beings of nature have that same force inside us. A force that wants us to grow and create further.

'So, whether you like it or not, growth is an important aspect of achieving your full potential. By all means, move at a pace that works for you, but keep moving, keep growing. Some degree of forward momentum is what matters.

'Although I'm not a religious person … ,' said The Oracle, continuing his line of thought. ' … spiritual, yes, but religious, no … one of my favorite quotes does happen to be from the Gospel of Thomas, which says, "If you bring forth what is within you, what you bring forth will save you. If you do not bring forth what is within you, what you do not bring forth will destroy you."

'I seriously love that sentiment,' said The Oracle, 'and I find it very helpful to think of growth as the process of bringing forth what's inside us. With that frame of reference, hopefully it's easy to see how growth is a good thing and not a bad thing. But let me explain further.'

He got up from his chair and wrote the words Hide, Survive, Strive and Arrive on the whiteboard, each within a series of arrows flowing left to right. Below those words he then matched each with the headings from the previous diagram: Embryo, Child, Adult, Sage. One after the other.

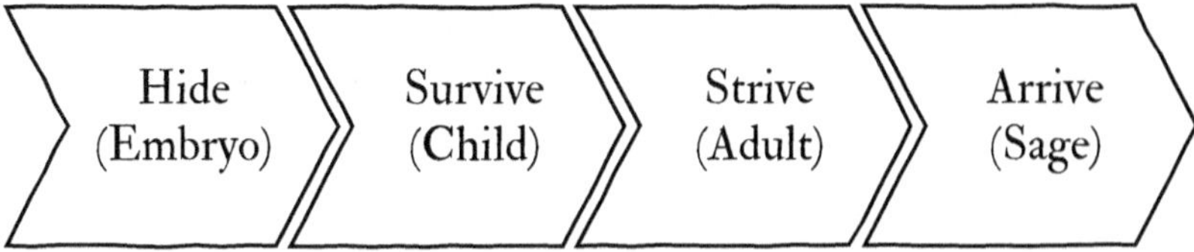

'To live a remarkable life, you will need to embark on what's often referred to as the "hero's journey"', explained The Oracle.

'In ancient mythology this was often portrayed as the search for the Holy Grail, although the famed Grail is not a physical object or treasure, as most would assume. No, the search is actually an inward journey taken in the external world, and the Holy Grail is the discovery of the *spirit* that lies within. At which point you are reunited with your divine nature and discover that you, and what a lot of people like to refer to as God, are, in fact, one and the same!

'Now that's an exciting discovery I'm sure you would agree, so I hope you can appreciate what all the fuss has been about throughout the ages – why the Holy Grail has been such a coveted treasure.

'Advancement is not easy, however,' warned The Oracle. 'Over the years, I've noticed that people typically get stuck in one of the three earlier phases, not making it to the coveted final phase of *Arrive.*'

There was some more uncomfortable shifting in seats as people contemplated each heading and where they might sit on the spectrum. I now suspected I had not even moved beyond Survive and certainly didn't like the Child label that accompanied it.

'Ah, I sense some trepidation,' said The Oracle, playfully wringing his hands together. 'This should be fun,' he said, feeding off the heightened vitality in the room.

'Some of you will most definitely be *Hiding* from life,' he challenged, pointing to the first phase of his diagram, 'although you won't want to admit it.' This drew a few more nervous murmurs from a large portion of those present.

'That is, you continue to shelter in the comfortable and the known. Unwilling to stray from the comfort of your daily routines. You have not yet fully ventured into the world, breaking away from the familiar to walk your own unique path. You have not been courageous enough to make yourself vulnerable and welcome uncertainty into your life.

'This is not a new phenomena though,' said The Oracle by way of reassurance. 'If I recount the following verses from Rumi's poem *Wean Yourself,* written sometime in the 13th century, you will realize we have been facing the same predicament for more than 700 years. So, don't be too hard on yourself if you fall into this category.

> *Think how it is to have a conversation with an embryo.*
> *You might say, 'The world outside is vast and intricate.*
> *There are wheatfields and mountain passes,*
> *and orchards in bloom.*
>
> *At night there are millions of galaxies, and in sunlight*
> *the beauty of friends dancing at a wedding.'*
>
> *You ask the embryo why he, or she, stays cooped up*
> *in the dark with eyes closed.*

Listen to the answer.

There is no 'other world.'
I only know what I've experienced.
You must be hallucinating.

The Oracle's recital was impressive, and the words thought provoking.

'Unacceptable!' he cautioned in a caring tone. 'No more of that. It's time to move on. This is no way to live your life.'

His challenge really struck a chord with me. *Bugger!* Maybe I was even less progressed than I had hoped. *Could it be possible that I hadn't even made it past the embryo stage?* Upon honest reflection I could see how I was guilty of staying cooped up in the dark with my eyes closed. I mean, the days, weeks and months were slipping past and wasn't really venturing into the unknown. I wasn't depressed or anything, I was just stuck.

Clearly, I needed to change my ways; I could see that now. The Oracle was right. Life can be extraordinary, but most of us shy away from the opportunity to truly shine because it means stepping out of our comfort zone. I realized I would have to do a better job of welcoming the uncertainty of the path less trodden.

Pointing to the second phase, **Survive**, The Oracle then continued: 'On the other hand, some of you will have taken that first step away from the familiar and the known, and now find yourself here in Survive. Well done on your progress. I appreciate that would have taken a lot of courage. I also appreciate that as you find yourself facing what feels like an endless array of challenges, being knocked from pillar to post, struggling to live from paycheck to paycheck, you are probably asking yourself why you ever bothered to venture out in the first place.'

There were nods and murmurs from the room, indicating that many present found themselves in that exact situation. I was glad to hear others were also feeling challenged.

'Well, don't give up, I say,' said The Oracle. 'As Churchill once said, "if you are going through hell, keep going". It *is* worth it. You are on your way to claiming the Holy Grail. This phase will eventually pass if you persist.'

The Oracle paused and smiled at us, appreciating he just made something quite daunting appear quite easy.

'Moving on, I have no doubt some of you will have already pushed through the Survive phase and emerged victorious,' he said with an air of encouragement. 'You now find yourself striving onwards and upwards. Intent on mastering the world.

'In this **Strive** phase you are unstoppable – progressively obtaining every object you desire and no doubt deriving enormous satisfaction and a sense of achievement from this. You are flying along, and nothing seems to be able to hold you back. It certainly appears you're on the path to living a remarkable life.

'And you are. That progression is not easy. It would have taken a lot of persistence to ultimately prevail and move beyond mere survival. An ability to visualize yourself living a different life, despite the most challenging circumstances. So, congratulations to you – *in part!*'

There was a moment's pause as The Oracle's rebuke sunk in.

'At the risk of taking the wind out of your sails, although you have done well to make it this far, this is not a place you want to stay.'

That was an interesting thought, and he had the room's attention.

'While Strive might feel like the place to be, it's a hoax,' asserted The Oracle. 'A deception. A swindle of the grandest scale. Here you remain far too susceptible to fear, stress, anxiety, greed and power to ever be truly happy. Here, you are not yet true to who you really are.

'The trick, therefore, is to actually go beyond Strive and enter the final stage. When you do this, you enter the realm of heaven on earth – the world of transcendence, of enlightenment.

'As I mentioned earlier, this is the Holy Grail. The discovery of the *spirit* that lies within. In **Arrive** there is no "me"; just "we".

Here you become a rare and precious being. You leap to an entirely different level, and a depth, meaning and significance will return to your life. You not only become a better version of yourself, you will transcend your previous self entirely. You will awaken to your true nature and, as a result, an innocence, beauty and sweetness that are not of this world will shine through you.

'To get there you will need to confront many new challenges and face your fears, but that's what makes this journey so exciting and rewarding. Take it and you will end up in a very different place. A good place. A remarkable place. *Arrive* is a truly beautiful place to be, so I encourage you all to move there and make it home, without delay.'

The Oracle paused, and we eagerly awaited his next thought. 'I cannot think of a better way to make this next point,' he said, 'so I'll just come out and say it.

'Soon you will be dead,'

he declared with the utmost gravity. 'There's no denying it; your life is truly fleeting. In the meantime, however, you have a job to do. You need to live your life. And live it well!

'The challenge you face, therefore, is life, not death. I appreciate that is the opposite of what most people think,' he said, 'but death is a given and does not set you apart from others.

'The big unknown is not *life after death* as most would have you think, but rather *life before death*. That is the mystery that must be solved. The real challenge is *living*, or, more specifically, *how to live your life*. That's what makes all the difference. That's what makes you unique.

'Jean-Paul Sartre, the great French philosopher, once said, "Everything has been figured out, except how to live!"

'Well, it's my intention for you to leave here tonight knowing exactly *how to live*. Most people are not nearly as successful and happy as they ought to be, but we can fix that.'

At that promise, I felt a great peace descend over me. Like the arrival of a much-anticipated blanket on a cold winter's night, the idea that help was on its way bathed me in comfort and warmed me to the core. I could sense that The Oracle had the answers I needed. He cradled my future ever so gently in the palm of his hand, and somehow I knew I could trust him to tread lightly and treat it well.

A very small change can make a very big difference

'My grandmother used to say,' continued The Oracle, '"If only you could put an old head on young shoulders." In my youth it seemed like such a ridiculous proposition. Even if it were possible, what benefit could it possibly achieve? Well now, as an *old* head, I see things differently and the benefits are significant indeed!

'The world in which we live, like most closed systems, is very sensitive to the starting conditions. A tiny difference in the "push" you receive at the beginning will cause a big difference to where you end up. Or, put another way, a very small change in trajectory at this stage of your life can make a very, very big difference in destination.'

That thought really struck a chord with me. I could visualize exactly how that could play out. I pictured my life as a projectile of some sort and how the right, albeit slight, change in trajectory now would result in me arriving at a totally different destination. The difference between a remarkable life and an ordinary one. I could now see how much was really at stake here tonight. How what I did now, this very evening, could actually change everything.

This could be the start of a very different future, I thought excitedly to myself.

'While the name of the game may appear to be dog-eat-dog,' continued The Oracle, 'and all about survival of the fittest, there is actually a much more collaborative and vastly more powerful system at play in the universe.

'And this is where things begin to get interesting. Really interesting,' said The Oracle. 'You see, people don't fail, it's their system that fails them!

'Success is not the byproduct of chance but rather the outcome of a system. Success and happiness do not require a miracle, they simply require a commitment to a small number of steps.'

Knockout!

I really liked that thought. That was not something I had heard before, but I really liked where this was heading.

'Catastrophe aside, failure to achieve happiness and success in life will therefore usually only mean one of two things,' continued The Oracle. 'Either you don't have a system or the system you are following is the wrong one.'

The system

'If you think about that for a moment, this opens up all manner of possibilities to the average person if they are seeking a remarkable life. If success can be the outcome of a relatively dependable, repeatable system; then the secret to life, the key to untold health, wealth and happiness, becomes the answer to one very simple question ...

What is the system?

'Well, here is the answer to that question ... '

The Oracle held up both hands high in the air with nine fingers protruding strongly.

'Nine things,' he said.

'First, I have committed to a divine and audacious intention.

'Second, I have embraced a new set of limitless beliefs.

'Third, I act in alignment with my virtuous Code of Conduct.

'Fourth, I rest knowing what I seek is already mine.

'Fifth, I have immersed myself in the seven great love affairs.

'Sixth, I am doing my Great Work.

'Seventh, I practice the 10 steps of perfect health and transcendence.

'Eighth, I have secured my financial freedom by implementing the seven laws.

'Ninth, I stay on track, leverage myself and enjoy the journey.'

Seems like quite a lot to do, I thought to myself.

'Now don't be overawed by this challenge either,' said The Oracle, as if sensing my hesitation.

'I call this the *Ninefold Path*, and you are more than capable of mastering it. In fact, the biggest problem I find is not the difficulty of the task but the fact that people only ever attempt to take on one or two aspects of the challenge.

'They might for instance set their sights purely on wealth creation and wonder – three marriages and seven estranged children later – why they failed so dismally at love. Or they may make business domination their objective only to find that although they have created a large and successful enterprise, their health teeters on a knife edge.

'Don't do that to yourself,' begged The Oracle in a surprising show of emotion. 'Commit to the entire *Ninefold Path* and you'll look back on a life well lived with pride and no regrets. Do this and you will have the very best opportunity to achieve your full potential. Do this and you are very unlikely to die with the music still inside you.'

Resistance to change

'The struggle in all of this is not the magnitude of the challenge but that we are wired to resist change. Even positive change. Our biology is designed to preserve the status quo, so as to maintain continuity. Given there are millions of things that need to be occurring in our body at any moment to keep us functioning, resistance to change is a natural phenomenon designed to keep us alive. But it will also be our death if we don't overcome it. Therein lies one of life's great paradoxes.'

The irony was not lost on me – the idea that what was designed to keep us alive would also be the cause of our death was indeed surreal.

'Entrepreneurship has been described as "living a few years of your life like most people won't, so you can spend the rest of your life like most people can't", said The Oracle. 'The challenge that now awaits you mirrors that philosophy to a tee. If you live a few months of your life like most people won't, you can spend the rest of your life living like most people really, really want to – but can't.'

That was a really exciting thought. I scribbled down his ninefold process furiously to capture the key points before he moved on.

1. I have committed to a divine and audacious intention.

2. I have embraced a new set of limitless beliefs.

3. I act in alignment with my Code of Conduct.

4. I rest knowing what I seek is already mine.

5. I have immersed myself in the seven great love affairs.

6. I am doing my Great Work.

7. I practice the 10 steps of perfect health and transcendence.

8. I have secured my financial freedom by implementing the seven laws.

9. I stay on track, leverage myself and enjoy the journey.

As it turned out, I needn't have been so worried about keeping up, as The Oracle seemed to have no intention of moving forward. Instead, he simply beamed at each of us in turn, taking the audience into his being, one after the other.

'Do you have any questions?' he finally asked, breaking the long silence.

Thankfully, a young woman in the front row raised her hand quickly and said, 'Would you mind expanding on each of the nine points so we can understand them better?'

'Of course,' replied The Oracle. 'I had every intention of doing that, but thanks for the prompt,' he added with a smile.

Part Two

THE SOLUTION

Step One

I HAVE COMMITTED TO A DIVINE AND AUDACIOUS INTENTION

The Oracle took a moment to collect himself and reconnect with his surrounds. He looked back out across the gathered audience with perceptible eagerness.

'At the risk of appearing a little geeky, can I just say how excited I am about this first step,' he said. 'It really is the start of something very special.'

It did appear that The Oracle would literally burst at the seams if he wasn't able to relieve himself quickly of what was on his mind. *His childlike enthusiasm is rather endearing and somewhat addictive*, I thought to myself as I shifted to the edge of my seat in anticipation of what was to follow.

'Many would have you believe that the life we live is either this random game of chance or a choreographed event, presided over by a central God-like figure. Yet, neither could be further from the truth,' contended The Oracle.

'No. Life is neither random nor choreographed. Instead, there is a reliable process of cause and effect that determines how the world works and what you are likely to receive. A process that you can use to your advantage!'

The Oracle remained silent, scanning the room for signs of life.

'I do hope at this point you're starting to get very excited,' he said, observing the group with interest, 'for we are touching on something rather extraordinary here!

'You see, there is a field of intelligent substance from which all things are made,' explained The Oracle. 'Which, in its original state, permeates, penetrates and fills the interspaces of the universe. This substance is the basic building block of the world as we know it, and *you're swimming in it!*' declared The Oracle.

'In fact, if it didn't already exist, you would be trying to invent this substance,' said The Oracle enthusiastically. 'But it does exist! You don't need to invent this miracle substance, because you are already immersed in it.

'Some people refer to this substance as God; I prefer to use the term *spirit*. What's more important than the name, however, is what's possible once we become aware of its presence.

'What do I mean by that? Well, we can cause the thing we desire to be created by impressing our thoughts upon this spirit. A thought placed in this spirit produces the thing that is imagined.'

Sensing the importance of this, I jotted down the concept ...

There is an intelligent substance

from which all things are made,

which, in its original state, permeates, penetrates

and fills the interspaces of the universe.

We can cause the thing we desire to be created

by impressing our thoughts upon this spirit.

'While your intention will not instantly manifest,' continued The Oracle, 'which is fortunate in many circumstances,' he said chuckling to himself, clearly reimagining some inappropriate thoughts of the past, 'it will put the process into motion.

'Now I hope you appreciate just how extraordinarily fortuitous it is to have access to this substance?' questioned The Oracle. 'But only if you are actually using it,' he added. 'Only if you are making use of this potential. Otherwise, it's a rather wasted opportunity,' he concluded with a look of dejection, seeking to hold us to account.

'In this regard I am reminded of the two young fish swimming along, who happen to meet an older fish swimming the other way. He nods at them and says, "Morning, boys. How's the water?" As they swim on, one of them eventually looks over at the other and says, "What the hell is water?"'

The audience broke out in laughter.

'Funny, right?' said The Oracle. 'But also, insightful and pertinent. Same for us. We are submerged in this intelligent substance, but most of us aren't even aware of its presence, let alone using it to our advantage.

'You see, life is not a game of chance. It is a game of probability. While lady luck definitely has a role to play, you can still stack the likelihood of success significantly in your favor.'

The key to unlocking life

I contemplated what had been said and realized this was the secret I had been looking for – the key to unlocking my life. If this were true – if there was, in fact, a dependable, repeatable process I could apply to achieve the results I desired – then the ramifications were truly extraordinary. But why didn't I already know this?

'Now this is quite a revelation,' said The Oracle in a serious manner, once again apparently anticipating my thoughts, 'so I hope you fully appreciate its significance: with this knowledge it becomes possible to see how you are both unlimited and all powerful. A very different perspective to what most people believe; I'm sure you will agree?' offered The Oracle enquiringly.

'You can make things wonderful for yourselves by using this deliberate and reliable process of creation. *I will believe it when*

I see it is how most people think. And yet the reality is the opposite – *you will see it when you believe it.*'

I really liked that distinction, and reflected that I had myself become far too skeptical and more likely *only to believe it when I see it.* I felt myself opening up once more to the miraculous nature of life and was thankful for the opportunity to do so.

'You have the capacity to produce your own heaven or hell on earth, right here and now,' said The Oracle, stopping for a moment to allow the point to hit its mark.

'How so? Well, you are the creator not the victim. You can create what you want to create; you can receive what you want to receive; you can become what you want to become. You can manifest that perfect creation that lies dormant inside you.

'While you may be heavily influenced by your genes, your past, your environment and your existing personality, you are not determined by them. You are not a product of your past. You are a product of the thoughts and actions you take from this point forward.

'Once you realize this it becomes much easier to have faith, to lose all doubt and fear. Knowing this should help to produce a relaxed confidence in your future, no matter how challenging your present circumstances.

'But, let me repeat that,' said The Oracle, 'as I don't want any of you to miss its significance. As humans, you are blessed with the unique ability to visualize yourself living a different life, to imagine any future you desire, and then make that a reality, no matter how challenging your present circumstances.

'So, don't squander that power on hollow escapism,' encouraged The Oracle. 'Do not use this extraordinary gift – your imagination – as a tool to simply escape your present reality; use it as a bridge to *build* a new reality.

'But what should your new reality be? What should you ask for? What should your new story, your intention be? To answer

that question, let's begin by asking ourselves another very important question. What is truly essential in life?'

No one responded.

'No, seriously,' said The Oracle, making it clear he needed an
answer from the audience. 'What do you think truly matters?'

'Love.' 'Money.' 'Your health ... ' were the first fledgling
responses from the audience.

'Brilliant, but keep it going if you have more,' he said, rising to
his feet and capturing the comments in a large thought bubble
on the whiteboard, as a flood of comments now ensued from the
crowd.

They rolled forth: your car, buying a house, your job, people's
opinions, the cost of petrol, and on and on it went.

'That's great,' he said, capturing all the thoughts and adding
a somewhat sad looking stick figure under the thought bubble
before turning back to face the group.

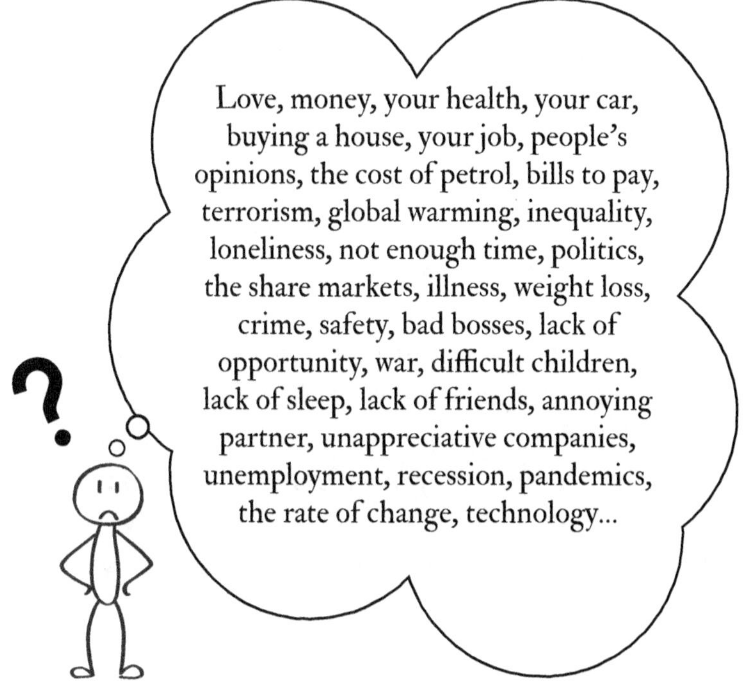

'If our first step requires you to commit yourself to a divine and audacious intention, there certainly appears to be a lot that you consider important,' said The Oracle.

'Thank goodness your thoughts don't appear as bubbles over your heads in the real world, is all I can say,' he added playfully, 'or you would all be committed.'

Although this comment provoked some laughter from the group, the point was well taken. We were clearly weighing ourselves down with a host of potentially unnecessary concerns.

'Please don't make the mistake of focusing on the wrong things in life,' said The Oracle. 'Life is much simpler than you think! That's one thing my work with numerous young adults over the past decade has taught me – far too many of you see life as this mass of confusing, conflicting demands. Yet, there are only a few things that really matter, and you can be highly successful in each – I have no doubt about that – once you know how.

'What are those few things? Well, contrary to what the marketers would like you to think, it will not matter what you owned or how beautiful you looked. In the end, it will only matter what you gave, who you loved and how you enriched the lives of others.

'Furthermore – and this is a really liberating thought – there is no shortage of these few things. There is no scarcity. They are available in absolute abundance. While that may not be true of all things, it is true of the things you will need to make your *remarkable* life a reality.

'The exciting thing about that, of course, is the realization you can live a remarkable life without impacting negatively upon the greater good. In fact, the opposite is true. By following the system I am revealing here tonight, you will not only create a remarkable life for yourself but in the process you will help to save the planet and all those living on it. How's that for an outcome? Who could ask for more?'

Finding and achieving your purpose

'Mark Twain once said: "The two most important days in your life are the day you are born and the day you find out why." Let's now agree on the *why*, shall we?' said The Oracle. But not before he took a moment to rearrange himself on the stool once more, breathe in deeply and seemingly center himself.

'Firstly,' he began, springing back to life, 'in terms of purpose, I believe you are here to realize your full potential, **and help all those you come into contact with to realize theirs.**

'What I particularly like about this purpose,' suggested The Oracle, 'is the way it recognizes the need to take care of your own needs but then quickly moves to a focus on helping others.

'As wanting animals, it is unrealistic for us humans to rid ourselves of desire: wanting more is fundamental to human nature. What we can do, however, is turn our desire for wanting more into a desire for wanting more for others. A desire to help others achieve their goals.

'So, if you don't already have something better, I would suggest you adopt that as your purpose for now. You can always refine it in the future.

'How do you achieve that purpose? Well, you achieve that by focusing on the *five* things that really matter. Let's capture these as your ***Vision of Perfection*** and it looks something like this ...

'First, *I love and am loved*, for it is truly love that makes the world go around. It is first and foremost through love and in love that we will find the extraordinary life we seek.

'Second, *I do my Great Work*. Deliver a unique and highly valued product or service that helps others to achieve their goals. Something that people would mourn the loss of if it no longer existed.

'Third, *I maintain a healthy body and mind and have reconnected to the spirit*. More on that later,' said the Oracle with a gleam in his eye.

'Fourth, *I have secured my financial freedom.* As most of you are fortunate enough to already be enjoying the other basic freedoms of life, the key is to have enough money to do what you need to do, when you want to do it.

'And, finally, *I enjoy the journey*, because the journey is far more important than the destination.'

The Oracle drew another thought bubble into which he wrote the Purpose and Vision of Perfection which collectively made up his suggested intention. The stick figure he drew below the bubble was now smiling, clearly appreciating the simplicity.

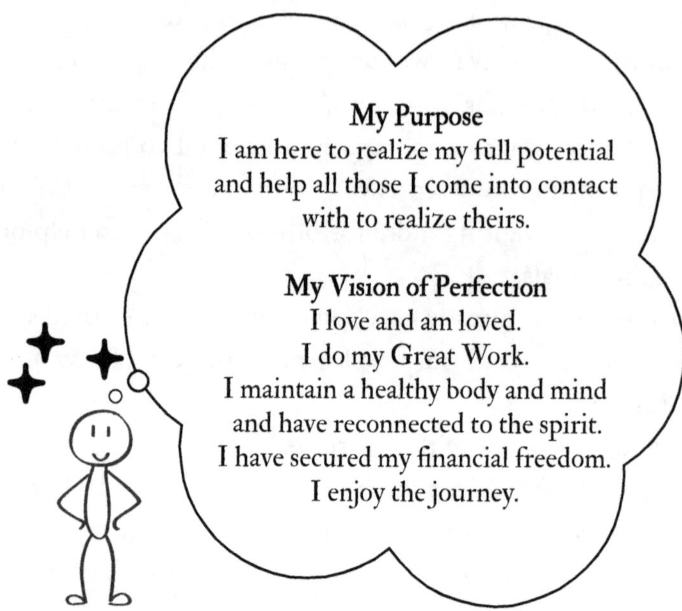

'As you have probably worked out already,' The Oracle continued, 'happiness is not something that can be pursued directly. Do that and it will continually evade you. No, happiness is a byproduct, the side effect, the outcome of a meaningful life. The end result of working on these five things.

'And make no mistake,' he said with a passionate tone, 'you deserve to be happy and you should expect to be happy! There is no need to be a martyr here. Life may be challenging but it can still be joyous!'

I wrote the purpose and the Vision of Perfection in my book:

My Purpose:

I am here to realize my full potential and help all those

I come into contact with to realize theirs.

My Vision of Perfection:

I love and am loved.

I do my Great Work.

I maintain a healthy body and mind and have reconnected to the spirit.

I have secured my financial freedom.

I enjoy the journey.

As I looked this simple statement over, I felt a surge of excitement. This really did simplify things a great deal and the words certainly appeared to capture the things that I wanted most. I imagined myself living true to my purpose and having achieved all five intentions and it felt both liberating and incredibly satisfying.

The Oracle continued, his words bringing me back to the present: 'This first step is all about producing a meaningful and coherent statement of intent. Did you know the reason most people fail to achieve their goals in life is they don't set them in the first place?' he asserted.

I hadn't heard that before, but now thinking about it, I could see the possibility and how easy it would be to fall victim to. I mean, here I was about to make the same mistake in my own life. Hell, I was already at least a quarter of the way through my own life without ever really having sat down and worked out what it was I truly wanted. Bloody hell! *I certainly needed this wake up*, I thought.

'You can't afford to make that simple mistake,' counseled The Oracle.

'That's why we begin with the end goal in mind. You see, life is best lived backwards. When scientists first decided to put a man on the moon, they didn't think – what do we need to do to get them there? They did the reverse. They imagined a successful landing and then worked their way backwards. We need to do the same. We need to start with what we want to ultimately achieve and be known for, and then work our way backwards.

'And you need to be definite in relation to that intention,' said The Oracle. 'As you can appreciate, an unaimed arrow will rarely hits its target, so be crystal clear on what you're seeking and hold that intention in your mind from one day to the next.

'Furthermore, you need to focus on what you want, *not* what you don't want in life. That's a really important distinction, so please make sure you understand its significance. A lot of people neglect its importance. If your focus is **not** being poor, **not** getting sick and **not** ending up in a disastrous relationship, then you will end up poor, you will get sick and you will end up in a disastrous relationship. That's exactly what you will get. The thing you focus on!

'As for the *divine* aspect of this intent? Well, that ensures that what you ask for comes from the real you, the true self, the spirit rather than the ego or false self – the heart not the head.

'The issue being,' explained The Oracle, 'that intentions originating from the ego are motivated by either fear or greed, and are therefore unlikely to be aligned to your unique destiny. In turn, they're unlikely to be achieved.

'On the other hand, intention born of the spirit, what I refer to as *divine* intention, cannot fail to materialize, as these intentions have within them the means of their own fulfillment. They can be trusted and are within your reach.

'In short, divine intentions place you in alignment with the world, which will in turn mobilize itself toward the fulfillment of your desires, which also means the answers you seek, the strength you require and the resources you need will all be there when you need them. I cannot guarantee you the same outcome where the whims of the ego are concerned.'

The Oracle shifted in his seat, straightening his back and relaxing his shoulders. I naturally did the same.

'As for being *audacious*, well, that's your opportunity to have a meaningful impact on the world. To leave it a better place, to make a difference.

'You can be one of the people who solves the world's problems. Don't settle for a life that is less than the one you are capable of living.

'As the great Muhammad Ali taught us, if your mind can conceive it, and your heart can believe it, then you can most definitely achieve it!

'I love that saying,' said The Oracle, rolling his shoulders and ducking clear of an imaginary punch with surprising agility, mimicking a boxer's warmup routine before a match. People responded enthusiastically. 'I can see I'm not alone in admiring the great man,' he said happily.

'You know, each and every one of you in this room also has the capacity to be truly great, to be successful, to be admired and respected by others. Within you is the power to help lift the world out of mediocrity.

'That's an exciting thought,' said The Oracle, 'and if you think you're too small to have an impact, remember what it's like going to bed with a mosquito in the room.'

Laughter erupted from the crowd. 'Ha, I can tell you know what I'm talking about,' he said, pointing at various members of the audience. 'I have a point, don't I? If something as small as a mosquito can make a difference, surely so can you.

'Young Athenians of old would take an oath to leave their country greater and superior before they died. It was this individual commitment to improve society for others that led to a civilization we still revere and marvel at today,' suggested The Oracle.

'I encourage you to do the same!' he said. 'Pledge that your life will amount to something, that it will have an impact, that you will make a difference. Roll up your sleeves and get involved in *life*. Do not plan to simply witness the achievements of others: make your own mark.

'Be a teacher that inspires people, an artist that moves people, an actor that transforms reality, a scientist that cures disease, a healer that makes people well, an engineer that solves problems others have not, a gardener that reacquaints us with the healing power of nature, and a caregiver that improves the quality of people's lives.'

He lowered his voice and we all leaned in: 'Most people take small, reliable steps, but I encourage you to do more. Step outside your comfort zone.'

With that he leapt to his feet and walked to the side of the stage. 'If I take 30 linear steps, I will have traveled about 30 yards.' He walked 30 large paces across the stage and then turned to face us.

'This is the way we typically approach life. Small, incremental steps that help us make sense of the world,' he said.

'If instead I took another 30 steps, but each step was twice as long as the previous one – my first step was one yard, my second two, my third four – by the time I have taken my thirtieth step, does anyone know how far I will have traveled?' He paused, but no one was game enough to answer.

'About 26 times around the globe, folks! That's 32 *million* times more than the original number. How's that for audacious growth?'

By now, he had made it back to his seat. 'So, what's the moral of the story? Well, most people overestimate what they can do in one year and underestimate what they can do in 10. Begin to approach life with a more audacious point of view. Make it your goal to get twice as good each year, then after only 10 years, you will be 1024 times as good as you were when you started. Now, that's one hell of an improvement!'

Letting this concept take hold, The Oracle sat quietly facing the attentive crowd. In the silence I wondered what audacious might look like for me. On that I was unsure, but at least I felt comfortable I now knew where to start.

'So, to recap, we are talking about *how to live* your life.' The Oracle got on his feet once more and drew the sketch of a young male and female, above which he wrote: Step 1: I have committed to a divine and audacious intention. And then he jotted down both the purpose and the five key intentions that captured the intention.

> **Step 1: I have committed to a divine and audacious intention**
> I am here to realize my full potential and help all those I come into contact with realize theirs. I will do this by: Loving and being loved. Doing my Great Work. Maintaining a healthy body and mind and reconnecting to the spirit. Securing my financial freedom. Enjoying the journey.

Universal appeal

A hand immediately shot up and a man directly in front of me commented, 'I really like your five intentions and find they resonate deeply, but aren't an individual's goals a personal thing and therefore something we can't generalize about?'

'Well, yes and no, or, more precisely, no and yes,' replied The Oracle.

'No in the sense that all the work I have done to date with people has taught me that, deep down, we are all very similar and want the same things in life. So, the purpose and these five core intentions tend to have universal appeal for all of us.

'But yes, in the sense that you will most definitely need to personalize what these intentions look like for you at a more granular level. The amount of money you require to achieve financial freedom, and what your Great Work shall be, are, for instance, things that will vary significantly from one person to another. One person may be content living on $50,000 a year, the other requires $500,000.

'In that regard, I agree you will need to ensure that your intention reflects your own unique story. We all have our own destiny, so yes, you need to define what is required to be true to your plan – and no one else's.

'To do that you simply need to add a third dimension to the intention. What we call a Vivid Descriptor. This is your compelling 10-to-30-year goal that links back to your **Purpose** and **Vision of Perfection** but adds a sufficient level of detail to bring it all to life. It needs to be something that excites and energizes you even if it appears outrageous at first.

'Use the Vivid Descriptor to describe *exactly* what it is you want to achieve under our five key headings. What heaven on earth might look like for you, keeping in mind that the only person you are destined to become is the person you decide to be.

'So be very clear on that. This is your opportunity to become self-contained, self-motivated and ruled by your own definition of success, avoiding forever hereafter the lethal and debilitating trap of always comparing yourself to others.

'We live in a world where far too many people are trying to prove things to people they do not respect and trying to obtain things they do not really need. This *Vivid Descriptor* becomes the only valid reference point for you in life. An internal scoreboard.

'For that reason, I am loath to be too specific in describing what a Vivid Descriptor may look like for you,' explained the Oracle, 'because they are highly personalized things, but an example might be something like the following.'

The Oracle proceeded to talk through the following five headings:

1. **Love:** I have an incredibly fun, loving and supportive
   relationship with my partner and our beautiful children.
   I enjoy a very close relationship with my extended family and
   have a wonderful, small group of intimate friends that we
   journey together through life with.

2. **Healthy body and mind and reconnection to the spirit:**
   I keep myself fit, healthy and youthful. Through my daily
   practice of meditation and mindfulness I am in touch with my
   inner wisdom and allow it to guide me joyfully, peacefully and
   effortlessly through life.

3. **Great Work:** My work allows me to enrich the lives of others,
   while still leaving me plenty of quality time to spend with my
   family and loved ones, relaxing on the weekends and exploring
   the world each year, visiting new and interesting people and
   places.

4. **Financial freedom:** We have no personal debt. We live in a beautiful home in a nice suburb plus we have a lovely little beach getaway with wonderful ocean views. I drive a simple but reliable car that I replace every 10 years. The kids are getting a great education. We have a $x million share/property portfolio that provides $x in passive income per annum, providing us the freedom to live the life we want and help others less fortunate.

5. **Enjoy the journey:** While life is not without its challenges it is still incredibly fulfilling and enjoyable. I feel very fortunate to be alive.

The Oracle stopped. *Shit!* I thought to myself. That would be one hell of a life. Sure, I know it needs a little tweaking to make it mine, but I could see the potential for something quite remarkable here.

'See, this is a once-in-a-lifetime opportunity to write yourself a new story,' said The Oracle, continuing once the chatter in the room had died down. 'A bold, empowering and energizing new story that you will progressively turn into reality, using the *Ninefold Path*. Utilizing a predictable and reliable process, rather than relying on chance or luck.

'In summary, that's step one,' he said. 'I hope that adequately answers any questions?' to which the room appeared to nod as one indicating it was satisfied.

'Excellent, let's move on then,' said The Oracle, full of enthusiasm. 'We still have a lot to cover in the short time we have left. And the best is yet to come.'

Step Two

I HAVE EMBRACED A NEW SET OF LIMITLESS BELIEFS

'I could call this step *the lies we tell ourselves*,' said The Oracle when the room had fallen into silence, 'but I thought I would take a more positive slant, which is why I describe step two as *embracing a new set of limitless beliefs*.'

A profound influence

'Our beliefs, or the stories we tell ourselves, can have a profound influence on the quality of our life:

- "I am a victim ... "
- "Life isn't fair ... "
- "I am afraid ... "
- "I am frustrated ... "
- "I can't ... "
- "Other people control my life ... "
- "I am unable to get what I want and need in life ... "
- "The decisions I make usually turn out wrong ... "
- "I am unworthy ... "

- "I don't deserve to be happy … "
- "This will never last … "
- "People are jealous of me and try to bring me down … "
- "I am not supported … "
- "I can't trust anyone … "
- "I need to fight to survive … "
- "Life will ultimately let me down … "
- "All men are bastards … "
- "I'll never understand women … "
- "I can't control myself … "
- "I have an addictive personality … "
- "My opinion doesn't really matter … "
- "What I do isn't really important … "'

He took a moment to catch his breath.

That was quite a list, I reflected, and interestingly so many of them were alarmingly familiar to me.

'Remind you of anyone?' asked the Oracle. I went a light shade of pink, feeling that the question was somehow aimed specifically at me and I would have to publicly admit to my sins, before realizing he was not singling anyone out in particular.

'Lies, lies and more lies,' he said to the room with great passion. 'So many of the stories we tell ourselves are nothing but cruel lies, which soon become self-limiting beliefs and in turn our reality. If you think you can, you can, but if you think you can't, you can't.'

He shrugged.

'Think of that dear friend who believes they are not beautiful enough. Or that colleague who thinks they are not good enough. Or that person you admire who thinks they do not offer enough to be valued, so take their own life … when it's obvious to you and everyone else just how wrong they have got it.

'You see, our experience of life is a direct consequence of how we see the world. This is a sentiment captured beautifully by Ludwig Wittgenstein when he said: "A man will be imprisoned in a room with a door that's unlocked and opens inwards as long as it does not occur to him to pull rather than push."

'Many of us, myself included,' said The Oracle, 'need to continually revisit that door to see if it really is locked; or do we simply need to pull rather than push? Have we created a self-imposed prison for ourselves as a consequence of our limited beliefs?

'Why do hardships stifle one person and ignite the imagination and resourcefulness of another to rise above and move beyond? Well, one of the great realizations for me was coming to understand that we see the world as we are, not as it is.

'Contrary to what I used to believe; we are not looking at the world through the lens of a camera – taking in what exists. No. We are acting as a projector, projecting onto the world our preconceived idea of reality.'

I really liked that thought.

We see the world as we are, not as it is.

We are a projector, not a camera.

'Think of the traveler who comes upon an old farmer hoeing his field beside the road,' said The Oracle, changing pace. 'Eager to rest his feet, the traveler hails the farmer, who seems happy enough to talk for a moment.

'"What sort of people live in the next town?" asks the traveler.

'"What were the people like where you've come from?" replied the farmer.

'"They were a bad lot. Troublemakers all, and lazy, too. The most selfish people in the world and not one of them to be trusted. I'm happy to be leaving the scoundrels."

'"Is that so?" replied the farmer. "Well, I'm afraid you'll find the same sort in the next town."

'Disappointed, the traveler trudges on his way, and the farmer returns to his work.

'Some time later, another traveler, coming from the same direction, wanders towards the farmer, and they stop to talk. "What sort of people live in the next town?" the traveler asks.

'"What were the people like where you've come from?" replied the farmer once again.

'"They were the best people in the world. Hardworking, honest and friendly. I'm sorry to be leaving them."

'"Fear not," said the farmer. "You'll find the same sort in the next town."

The Oracle allowed the moral of the story to sink in. *That's a great story*, I thought to myself. And so true. I thought of all the times I had more than likely not realized the full potential of a situation because of the perspective I brought to it.

'The solution to your problems,' continued The Oracle, 'is rarely rearranging things on the outside. It's much more likely to require you to rearrange things on the inside. You really can alter your life by altering your beliefs. As Mahatma Gandhi taught us:

> *Your beliefs become your thoughts.*
> *Your thoughts become your words.*
> *Your words become your actions.*
> *Your actions become your habits.*
> *Your habits become your values.*
> *Your values become your destiny.*

'Whatever follows the words *I am ...* or *I don't have ...* will eventually become your reality. *I am not good enough, I don't have enough*, and on and on it goes,' explained The Oracle.

'Think about this old fable,' said The Oracle. 'A farmer finds an abandoned eagle's egg and puts it with his chickens. Soon the egg hatches. The young eagle grows up happily among the chickens. Whatever they do, the eagle does too. He thinks he is a chicken, just like them. Since the chickens could only fly for a short distance, the eagle also learnt to fly a short distance. He thought that was what he was supposed to do. So that was all that he thought he could do. As a consequence, that was all he was able to do. One day the eagle saw a bird flying high above him. He was very impressed. "Who is that?" he asked the hens around him. "That's the eagle, the king of the birds," the hens told him. "He belongs to the sky. We belong to the earth, we are just chickens." So the eagle lived and died as a chicken, for that's what he thought he was.'

This story really made an impact on me. I had definitely fallen into the trap of believing myself to be a small and limited chicken when in fact I could still be an eagle.

'If you think of your life as a tree,' said The Oracle, rising to his feet and sketching the outline of a tree on the whiteboard, 'then the beliefs you hold are the roots that feed the tree and support the trunk. They are the starting point of everything. Transformation will therefore require you to go all the way down to your rooted belief system. If change doesn't start there, the tree will easily topple.'

Twelve core beliefs

'As to what constitutes empowering beliefs, can I suggest twelve core beliefs that should resonate deeply with you. If not immediately, then hopefully at least by the end of the evening you will recognize their significance.'

He proceeded to outline them in turn ...

1. We are not naturally inclined to live a remarkable life – but a complete cure is available by following the *Ninefold Path*

'As humans our common state is one of suffering, misery, dissatisfaction, and a rather fleeting sense of happiness. We are inherently dysfunctional and operate under a veil of delusion, thereby missing the point of existence. But life is much simpler than we think. A complete cure is available, by following the *Ninefold Path*. There are only five things that really matter, and nine steps you need to take to make those five things a reality. You can have it all – health, wealth, and happiness – as there is no scarcity when it comes to these five things. They are available in absolute abundance. Your gain will not impact negatively upon the greater good. In fact, the opposite is true.

2. All is one – I therefore honor, love and serve all others and all of life

'The perception that we are separate is a delusion. The whole of life is one, the seen and the unseen, matter, and spirit. We are all part of one unbroken, unified, single whole despite the illusion of being a multitude of separate objects. All is one. What befalls one, befalls all. I am no better than anyone or anything and nothing is better than me. I have reverence for all life. There is no need to compete or triumph. Life is not a game to be won, but a journey where everyone can win. And the objective is not winning but ensuring the continuation of play. Cooperation and collaboration are the objective. There does not need to be a loser for me to be a winner. I therefore honor, love and serve all others and all of life.

3. The universe is governed by a divine intelligence that I can work with to accomplish anything I truly desire

'There is a spirit, an unmanifested energy, from which all things are made that permeates, penetrates and fills the interspaces of the universe. This is an intelligence far greater than myself, seeking beauty, seeking to co-create what is inside me. I can cause the thing I truly desire to be created by impressing my thoughts upon this spirit. A thought placed in this spirit will produce the thing that is imagined. I therefore work harmoniously in collaboration with the spirit. Co-creation is the name of the game. I clarify the intention, the spirit sets up the opportunity, and I conclude the process by taking the necessary action. Whatever I truly desire is close at hand. Anything that accords with my potential is possible. I am enough and have enough to be truly remarkable and live a remarkable life.

4. I am a necessary and important part of that divine intelligence – I therefore honor myself by bringing forth what is inside me without delay

'I am a rare and precious being. An important and necessary part of divine intelligence. A vehicle for divine expression. My essential nature is pure immortal, eternal energy. A manifestation of the divine in material form. I am not some small, insignificant speck within the universe. Quite the contrary – I am the universe, and the universe is within me. Each birth carries with it the possibility of change; I am one such possibility. It does not require work to become who I am, I simply need to get out of the way and allow myself to unfold. I no longer need to operate within the tribal mind. I am my own hero and leader. I have no master other than myself. There is no need to worship another. My destiny is not a secret. I will bring forth what is inside me without delay and become the hero I am destined to be.

5. Nothing is fixed – I can change the outer aspects of my life by changing the inner aspects of my life

'I am all powerful and limitless, able to go well beyond what I currently perceive to be the limits of my ability. I see the world as I am, not as it is. I am not looking at it through the lens of a camera, taking in what exists. I am acting as a projector, projecting onto the world my preconceptions. The world will change when I perceive it differently. Everything around me can be transformed. I can craft a new landscape in which to live my life – one that has not previously existed. I can leave the landscape of my past and ancestors behind – one formed in fear and duality – and claim a magnificent new heritage. My mind is like a garden – what I decide to grow there will determine the quality of my life. If I change the soil, I change what can grow. I do not need to rearrange things on the outside to flourish, just things on the inside.

6. I welcome challenges, setbacks, and failures along the way – they will only make me stronger

'Life does not promise to be fair. It will continually go up and down; it is both predictable and unpredictable; we get both what we want and don't want. I will experience setbacks and failures along the way. But none of that will stop me from enjoying the journey. Losing does not turn me into a loser; I am not worth less if I fail. That's all just part of the game. The obstacle is the way. I choose to be free and happy no matter what befalls me, to flourish on both the good and bad days. To be thankful for the hardships of the past and appreciate the world as it is, not as I would like it to be. I do not wish things were other than they are. I do not ask, *why me?* I simply ask, *what next?* I welcome challenges as learning experiences toward my inevitable, complete success. They are the best teachers and an opportunity for growth. They can all be handled. They will make me better. Looking back, I have no regrets. I can't 'should have'. 'If only' does not exist.

7. How I react in every circumstance is my choice – I am in control

'Although I cannot always control what happens to me, or how people act, I can always control how I respond. What happens is not as important as how I respond. How people treat me is their choice, but how I react is mine. I am not a victim. No one or no event can make me feel a certain way without my consent. My happiness is not dependent on external circumstance. The external world is not the cause of my suffering. I cannot blame others or events for how I am feeling or how I react. It's not the thing that upsets me, it's my judgment about the thing. The only thing upsetting me is my own imagination. I decide what story I tell myself about what has happened. I determine what's good or bad. I get to write my own history. I do not need to control external circumstance; I simply need to control myself. It's not a matter of, *I will be happy when* … , or, *if only you would* … I focus on controlling the controllable.

8. Both the world and I are impermanent – I therefore welcome both change and death into my life

'The true nature of the world is always moving, flowing, never resting, perpetual motion. What appears material is just immaterial vibrating energy – nothing is permanent. Everything, myself included, is continually changing. I therefore relax into that change and see the world afresh. Although I appreciate, welcome, and enjoy the material, it will never be my own, so I ensure the grip I have on it is light and gracious. I do not covet, nor cling to that which is transitionary, I simply receive but do not keep, knowing the most important things in life are immaterial. I am happy to give up any part of myself, as I continually evolve, until it is time to start afresh, totally afresh. That's how I view death: just another beginning. I have already died a thousand deaths and had a thousand births in this lifetime alone. I am born anew in every moment.

9. Love is the divine power – I therefore love myself, all others, the planet, and all I do

'Love is the thing of greatest importance. The highest goal to which we can aspire. It is love that makes the world go around, it is love that makes us beautiful. Love is a simple act that knows no bounds, something that I have the capacity to give in abundance and never run short of. It is the source of true happiness. A love of myself, my partner, my children, my friends and family, the planet, and all others without exception and without condition – every other living creature on this fair earth. I honor my family and love all I do. I have nothing to feel ashamed of or guilty about and I forgive myself for any wrongs. I form unions with people who support my development and release relationships that handicap my growth. I know I will get treated in life the way I teach people to treat me. No one can reject me but me.

10. I exist in a limitless ocean of health where age doesn't matter – my health span will match my lifespan – I am my own healer

'I am perfectly well, enjoying a perfectly strong and healthy body that is full of life and vitality. I do my work easily and with no end of stamina, never feeling tired or weak. There is no need to reject and deny disease – I simply need to be at one with perfect health. I know all internal functioning will be performed in a perfectly healthy manner. I know there is far more health power than disease power in both me and in the environment. I am my own healer and exist in a limitless ocean of health where age doesn't count.

The human body is the best machine ever made; it will continually rebuild itself with perfectly healthy cells. When any idea of disease or imperfect functioning enters my mind or body, I cast it out by returning to harmony with the conception of perfect health upon which the spirit that permeates and fills the tissues of my body will cause my body to be rebuilt with perfectly healthy cells.

11. The streets are paved in gold – there is no limit to my income, if I help others to achieve their goals

'My income will be determined by how many people I serve and how well I serve them. There are no limitations to what I can earn because I can always find more people to serve. The more lives I impact and the more value I create – the more money I can make. Anybody can build a great business because anybody can serve. There are therefore endless opportunities in the market to improve existing businesses or launch new ones as consumer wants and needs never cease to grow and the opportunity to satisfy that demand will be overlooked by existing companies. But I will need to make a deposit before I expect to receive any interest; I will need to place some wood on the fire before I can expect it to generate any heat. In short, my success will be determined by the extent to which I help others achieve theirs.

12. There is no need to be fearful or anxious – the universe is a friendly place – I can trust it has my back and make the rest of my life the best of my life

'Life is a wonderful adventure, full of hope and possibility. With no need for fear and doubt. The divine cannot be fearful or anxious. These feelings are simply a construct of the delusional self. There is no fear or anxiety in the world, only people thinking fearfully, anxiously. They are not real. I cannot be what I am not. I therefore relax, do my best, and enjoy the journey knowing my best will be good enough. The universe is a friendly place, it will conspire to help me. I don't need more of anything to be secure. I can trust the wisdom that created me, I can trust my instinct to guide me. My family of origin and those I interact with have been chosen to teach me the lessons I need to learn. I just need to take one step at a time, knowing that there are always miracles in the world, even when it seems dark. Things will ultimately go well for me.'

… The Oracle then paused, to allow us a moment to catch up and reflect.

That's quite a different way to look at the world, I thought to myself, and yet each belief felt surprisingly familiar in the sense that each somehow made immediate sense to me and connected very deeply. They were profoundly intuitive but, sadly, they were not something I could say I currently embraced. *There's clearly some work I need to do in this space*, I thought to myself, and welcomed the opportunity to do so.

The Oracle equally remained silent, deep in thought, before surging back to life: 'You know, they say it's often easier to correct a misbelief than adopt a truth,' he ruminated. 'Well if that's the case, then these are the misconceptions you need to correct:

- 'We are separate from one another and from nature.
- 'We should exert our dominion over nature.
- 'I am a physical being.
- 'Who I am is what I have and what I do.
- 'Who I am is what others think of me.
- 'I am powerless to truly make a difference.
- 'I am fundamentally flawed, somehow broken or imperfect.
- 'By succeeding I am being disloyal to and leaving behind people from my past.
- 'I am not totally loveable.

- 'I am not good enough.
- 'I don't have enough.
- 'You can't be happy all the time.
- 'Life wasn't meant to be joyous.
- 'There is so much that can go wrong with your health.
- 'There is much to fear and hate.

'Once again, lies, lies, lies,' said The Oracle with noticeable scorn. 'You can do way better than that. Let's add this second step to our Life Plan, shall we?' he then said, turning to the whiteboard and writing: Step 2: I have embraced a new set of limitless beliefs, and then added the words The 12 Core Beliefs underneath. The diagram now looked like this ...

Step 1: I have committed to a divine and audacious intention
I am here to realize my full potential and help all those I come into contact with realize theirs. I will do this by: Loving and being loved. Doing my Great Work. Maintaining a healthy body and mind and reconnecting to the spirit. Securing my financial freedom. Enjoying the journey.

'Looking a little lopsided, don't you think?' he reflected, and then turned back to address the room.

'Let's see if we can do something about that. Time for step three.'

Step Three

I ACT IN ALIGNMENT WITH MY VIRTUOUS CODE OF CONDUCT

The Oracle looked around the room, seeming to enjoy the building energy of those present. 'Our third step simply requires you to act in alignment with your virtuous Code of Conduct,' he said.

'This is all about character, your ethical nature, your personal credibility, the trust that others might reasonably have in you and your empathy towards others.

'For thousands of years, the development of character was the emphasis of a formal education, yet today such skills are rarely taught. I wonder why?' he said, lost in deep thought before bringing himself back.

'In a nutshell this step is recognizing that it's not about winning at all costs. You do not want to reach the end of life and look back with regret at the way you conducted yourself, with no time left to make amends. You want to be proud of the life you have lived, not just what you have achieved.

'Although this may mean you will have to pass up certain opportunities along the way, what you might lose in doing this will be well and truly justified by what you ultimately gain. The journey is far more important than the destination.

'That little difference between one person and another is really important,' continued The Oracle, 'so think carefully about what type of person you want to *be*.'

I considered my own journey to date and had to admit that I certainly didn't have a code of conduct I would be able to actually recite if someone asked me to. I was more likely to just take each situation as it came. I could see the benefit in it, however.

The A to Z of Life

'The intention here is very simple,' said The Oracle. 'Like the knights of old, you can develop a set of guidelines to guide you and ensure you are consistent and honorable in the quality of your day-to-day dealings with other people. While we all make mistakes, it's likely your errors will be far fewer if you provide yourself with some guidance, some parameters and some rules by which to live.

'This is what I refer to as the *A to Z of Life*.' The Oracle reached for a piece of paper at his side and held it high for all to see. 'I will give you all a copy of this now, but essentially it is a list of those behaviors I have found to be common in the lives of extremely successful and happy people.'

A stack of papers was handed around the room, and everybody took a copy. The Oracle gave us all time to read. Here is his *A to Z of Life*:

A is for **acceptance**. I surrender to the reality of the current circumstance – whatever it contains – as if I had chosen it. I do not approach the problem as though it should be different. I make it my friend and ally, not my enemy. This is not resignation; it is acknowledgement of the current reality. I accept, then act. *(vs **Resistance**)*

B is for always doing my **best** and wanting to be my **best**. Not being perfect, just doing my best in the circumstance and working hard to make my best continually better. If I have done my best, then I cannot have any regrets. This helps me to accept myself and cope with the criticism of others. *(vs **Perfectionism**)*

C is for **confidence** in myself, the goodness of others, the system, and the future. Knowing that no one can take away, delay, or stop what is mine. Knowing that the world will conspire to help me. That things will ultimately work out in the end. *(vs **Doubt**)*

D is for **discipline**. Doing those less pleasurable things that will result in a pleasurable outcome, as opposed to just doing what is pleasurable, whether I feel like it or not. It is the ability to delay gratification. Discipline is all about doing what is right versus what is easy, even if no one else is watching. *(vs **Impulsive**)*

E is for **emotional intelligence**. Self-awareness (knowing what I am feeling and why). Self-regulation (recognizing that between stimulus and response there is a space, and within that space is the power to choose my response). Self-motivation (taking action to pursue goals and complete tasks). Empathy (understand and appreciate others). (vs *Apathy*)

F is for being **fearless** and in time simply **fearing less**. Initially, feeling the fear and doing it anyway. Not running from pain or troubles, knowing it's what I don't face in life that controls me. But then in time simply fearing far less. Acknowledging the ultimate goal would be triumphing over fear altogether. *(vs **Fear**)*

G is for **gratitude**. The act of truly appreciating what I already have, no matter how big or small, despite wanting more.

I do not take the things I already have for granted; my family, the friendships, the roof over my head, the warm bed and clean water, the food on my table, my health and the opportunity to serve others. *(vs **Greed**)*

H is for **harmony**. To collaborate and co-create. To align with the current, to work with the nature of things, and find the path of least resistance, while ceaselessly and effortlessly flowing forward. When chaos is all around, to find the harmony within, not letting the internal flame flicker. Being actively calm, and calmly active. *(vs **Conflict**)*

I is for **ingenuity**. I do not accept the status quo. I seek to make things better. When faced with two imperfect options I come up with a third and better way that is a superior option, capable of meeting the objective without any compromise. In essence it's about having my cake and eating it too. *(vs **Compromise**)*

J is for **joy**. Finding the joy and seeing the humor in life. Not taking myself or life too seriously. Enjoying the journey for its own sake. Waking every morning excited and inspired about the new day and the opportunity it presents. When bad things happen, I only allow myself three minutes to be upset, before letting go and moving on. *(vs **Unhappy**)*

K is for **knowledge**. A thirst for new knowledge. Being the perpetual student, being curious. Always stretching, trying new things and acting in new and better ways. The art of continually evolving, improving and growing. Recognizing that others know things I don't, and that there is still so much to learn. *(vs **Fixed**)*

L is for **love**. Responding in all circumstance as love would. If I loved myself, if I loved you, if I loved what I was doing, how would I respond? I am kind and treat all with dignity. I assume every thought I send another is delivered instantly.

I know that it is never loving that hurts, it is not loving. *(vs* ***Judgment)***

M is for **modesty**. I know I am special, but no more special than anyone else. That my achievements are not so much *by* me, as *through* me. That I have been assisted greatly by the accomplishments of others whose shoulders I stand on. That my success is partly a result of my hard work but also the opportunities made available to me. *(vs* ***Hubris)***

N is for living in the **now**. I live in the precious present. I realize there are no ordinary moments and that the only time I have is now. I experience the moment that is passing through me. I lean in. I am part of what's going on. I turn what is unconscious conscious. I do not dwell on the past or worry about the future. I appreciate that I am born anew in every moment. *(vs* ***Unconscious)***

O is for being the **objective observer**. I do not take things personally. I am the detached silent observer. Aware of what is happening around me, receiving the pleasant without grasping and the unpleasant without judgment. I use quietness to escape the habits of normal perception and see things as if for the first time. *(vs* ***Attachment)***

P is for **persistence** and **patience**. The art of never giving up despite hardship, setbacks and failure. I thrive on the challenge without loss of enthusiasm, I am committed to long-term outcomes. I turn difficulties into post-traumatic growth, recognizing that what has been broken can emerge even stronger and more beautiful. *(vs* ***Give Up Easily)***

Q is for **questioning**. I never make assumptions. I clarify my thinking. I am circumspect and skeptical about what I am told, and less sure about what I think I know for sure. I seek out the essence or true nature of things and people, looking for the truth behind appearances, lifting the veil of misconception. *(vs **Naive**)*

R is for taking **responsibility** for how I am feeling, what has happened and what is happening in my life. Accepting that I have created every success and every failure to date. That I am the creator of both my pain and freedom. While I may not control fully what happens to me, every response is a choice. *(vs **Victim**)*

S is for **simplicity**. I keep life really simple by only focusing on the few things that really matter – and within those few things, only focusing on the few things that really matter. The 20% of activities that will deliver 80% of the outcomes. I always seek the simplicity that lies on the far side of complexity. *(vs **Complexity**)*

T is for **truthful talk**. I am impeccable with my word to myself and others. I speak with integrity to myself and others. I say only what I mean. I do not speak against myself or respond too harshly towards myself when things have not gone according to plan. I say what's right, no matter how painful that might be. *(vs **Dishonest**)*

U is for **uncertainty**. I welcome uncertainty and the unknown, and the adventure and mystery it brings. I realize that security cannot be 'sought', it is within the Self. I must take the first step even when I can't see the entire staircase. I recognize the road to success is paved with risks worth taking. *(vs **Risk Averse**)*

V is for **vulnerability**. I move through life with an open heart, that is never closed or withdrawn, despite the pain and anguish I have endured. I do not avoid pain or rejection. I realize any walls built to protect me will only become a prison. I therefore lean in, remain open, and let it all pass through me. *(vs **Closed**)*

W is for the peaceful **warrior**. I determine my path, honor my beliefs and live true to my values. I enter the daily battle anew with a peaceful heart and warrior spirit, willing to take the challenges of everyday life head on. I put myself out there, try my hardest, and reap the lesson, win or lose. Growing stronger and more skilful as I go. *(vs **Fragile**)*

X is for **xtreme**. I am audacious. I think big. I act boldly. I continually reset what's possible as I reach my previous goals. I do not merely adapt myself to the world, as I appreciate all progress depends on the unreasonable person. I do not merely settle for good, while there is still a chance to achieve the great or remarkable. *(vs **Reasonable**)*

Y is for saying **yes** to **you**. I bring more of myself to each day and every moment. I am true to myself, listen to my heart and follow my dreams. I define my own version of success. I do not seek external validation. I think beyond the confines of culture. I become whole, rather than perfect. Finding my unique voice. *(vs **Performer**)*

... and last but not least ...

Z is for **zeitgeist**. I understand that timing is everything. That what I do needs to be in alignment with the beliefs, the mood, the moral and cultural climate and spirit of the times. Good timing is invisible. I am therefore patient until the time is right, and then act accordingly. We can do anything, but we can't do everything at the same time.

Wow! That is quite a list, I thought to myself. I could see how following something like this could provide guidance in uncertain times, an internal reference point when feeling challenged, and generally help to make you a better person.

'Fearlessness or fear, gratitude or greed. The ones you choose to dance with determine the quality of your life,' continued The Oracle, when he sensed most people had read the list.

I liked that thought ...

Fearlessness versus fear. Gratitude or greed.

The ones you dance with determine your life.

'You can choose to master the entire A-to-Z list or simply parts of it. For me, they're all important in their own way.'

Returning to the whiteboard, he added another box, into which he wrote the words: Step 3: I act in alignment with my virtuous Code of Conduct. The A to Z of Life.

> **Step 1: I have committed to a divine and audacious intention**
> I am here to realize my full potential and help all those I come into contact with realize theirs. I will do this by: Loving and being loved. Doing my Great Work. Maintaining a healthy body and mind and reconnecting to the spirit. Securing my financial freedom. Enjoying the journey.

> **Step 2:**
> I have embraced a new set of limitless beliefs
> *The 12 Core Beliefs*

> **Step 3:**
> I act in alignment with my virtuous Code of Conduct
> *The A to Z of Life*

'That is our third step in understanding how to live. Now let's move on to step four. You will not want to miss this,' he said with great gusto.

'It's the most important step of all ... '

Step Four

I REST KNOWING WHAT I SEEK IS ALREADY MINE

The Oracle jumped right in …

'Having set yourself a divine and audacious intention, a new set of limitless beliefs and a virtuous Code of Conduct, the next thing we need to do is to be at one with that intent. To rest knowing that what you seek is *already* yours. Not wish or hope but *know*!' said The Oracle. 'There is a big difference.

'You see, as the great William James once taught us, you do not get what you *want* in life, but rather what you are.' I highlighted that point in my book as it seemed incredibly important and I had not come across it before.

> *We do not attract what we want in life,*
>
> *but, rather, what we are.*

'No. You cannot get what you have not yet become,' proffered The Oracle. 'For the purists among you this may be hard, but you've pretty well got to fake it until you make it. You've got to become one with the thing that you seek.

'Friedrich Nietzsche once said: "The visionary lies to himself, the liar only to others." Take this as confirmation that it's okay to lie to yourself at first. To see yourself as already having those things you don't yet have, and resting easy in the knowledge that if the desire comes straight from the spirit and is not driven by the ego's need for power and possession, they will all be yours in good time anyhow and therefore no longer a lie.

'Do this and you will set into play a repeatable process of creation.

'And if you don't; you won't,' he warned.

'Now this is a really important but subtle point,' emphasized The Oracle.

'One that can be very difficult to get your head around at first, so make sure you understand this fully,' he counseled. 'This step can often be the one step people get wrong, and if you do, you will put the whole system at risk.

'To make the intent we just defined under step one, two and three a subsequent reality, you need to be at one with that *intention*. You need to know that it is already yours. Like attracts like!

'Think of yourself as a TV or radio. Once you are properly aligned or tuned into the intended station you can begin to receive everything it has to offer. But you won't get anything until you are on the same frequency with what it is you seek. *Wanting* to be on the same frequency doesn't count. You must actually *be* on the same frequency. Once you understand this, everything will begin to change.'

Visualization

'This is what we call *visualization*, and it is a very common – albeit somewhat specialized – process undertaken by high-performing individuals to achieve their audacious goals. If you can see it, feel it and believe it, then you can become it. Once you become it then it is on its way.

'Allocate a time each morning to enjoy your intention, contemplating it, reveling in its delightful details. Loving it. Recognize that this is your new reality. Give thanks for it, both the elements you already have – that way you'll get to keep it – and the new.

'To help you make this a reality, adopt a new daily routine. This will ensure you allocate the necessary time to the process: time for visualization.'

The Oracle got up from his chair and sketched four ovals – one on top of the other – each intended to depict one the four components of a typical day. These he titled: Miracle Morning, Dynamic Day, Engaging Evening and Satisfying Sleep. He then drew a fifth oval off to the side, and at right angles to the original four, which he labeled Wonderful Weekend.

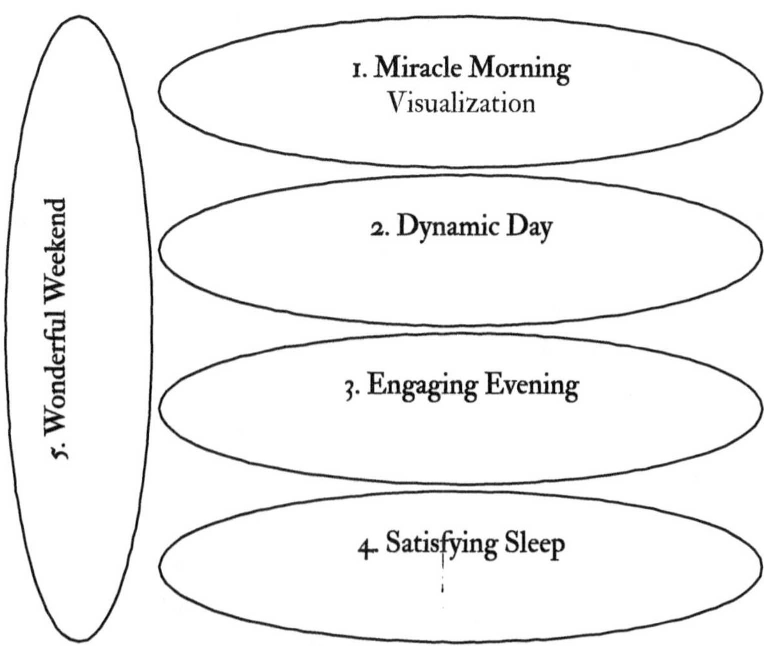

'This,' said The Oracle, pointing to what he had just created, 'is a way to imagine your typical week. For starters, as part of your Miracle Morning, take the time each morning to practice the art of *visualization*.

'The more you connect with your intention – and become one with it through the process of visualization, making it real by bringing out all its delicious detail, enjoying it in the moment – the quicker the transformation process will be.

'Don't ask for it, as that simply suggests you don't have it. The fact that it is yet to materialize is just a matter of process. Matter will follow mind as surely as day follows night. Like turning on a light switch and waiting for the lights to come on, the outcome is a guaranteed consequence of the act.

'Your new life is already present – even if some aspects of it are yet to come to fruition, change is on its way.'

I could see the subtlety or nuance here and now understood why The Oracle had warned at the outset that this is often the step that people get wrong.

Rest

'Before we finalize our discussion on step four, I would like to raise one final point,' said The Oracle, 'and that's the importance of the word *rest*. I *rest* knowing what I seek is already mine,' he said emphasizing the word rest as he spoke.

'The inclusion of this word is very intentional here,' he explained. 'It is a crucial precursor for this step four to play out in reality.'

Bugger, I thought, *I had hoped we had already covered the important elements of this step.* There was already a bit to get my head around here, nevertheless he had my attention.

'You may be familiar with the concept of fight or flight ... Well, what is less known to most, are the other two states we humans commonly display. One is freeze, which is rather self-explanatory,' said The Oracle.

I agree, I thought to myself. I was familiar with the idea of fight, flight or freeze.

'Interestingly, the fourth state is referred to as "rest & digest", or what I will simply refer to as rest,' explained The Oracle. 'This state actually sits at the opposite end of the spectrum to the other three. Opposite in the sense that the response of fight, flight and freeze are states induced by our sympathetic nervous system, which is there to ensure we respond appropriately to a perceived threat or danger. In any of these three states we are on high alert, pumped full of hormones to accelerate the heart rate, and able to do little more than focus on our immediate survival.'

The Oracle was on his feet with his right hand clasped to his heart as his eyes darted across the room, exploring our faces in what appeared to be a heightened state of fear. *He actually did quite a good job of suddenly looking fearful*, I reflected. So much so that I felt my own heart begin to race.

'The parasympathetic nervous system, on the other hand, is what turns off the sympathetic nervous system and restores the body to a calm and composed state,' said The Oracle as he sat down, closed his eyes, relaxed his shoulders, and took three deep breaths. The tension in the room fell away with him.

'This is the state of rest,' he said, once again opening his eyes, 'and it is only from this state that we can achieve anything of substance. It is only from this state that you can begin to make your intention a reality, thus the importance of this rather ordinary word making its way into our step four. Hopefully, you can now appreciate the significance of its inclusion. Until we reach this state of rest, all our internal resources are focused elsewhere'.

I get that, I thought to myself. I had felt his tension and state of alertness, which had immediately heightened my own, and then I had felt it fall away. I must admit no one had ever explained this fourth state of rest to me before, nor had I ever heard of the parasympathetic nervous system. This all made a lot of sense to me now. I could see why we can achieve nothing other than mere survival when we are in fight, flight or freeze mode, and the importance of rest as a state of being.

'The problem of course,' said The Oracle, 'is that most of us are spending the majority of our waking moments in fight, flight or freeze and extraordinarily little of our day at rest. So much of society is threatening or alarming to us: rushing to our next meeting, tomorrow's school test, tonight's homework, tomorrow's doctor's appointment, the weekend's semi-final, navigating through the peak-hour traffic, finishing that work assignment on time. On and on the list goes. If you think about it you could easily spend the vast majority of your life with your sympathetic nervous system activated.

'But that is neither healthy nor helpful,' counseled The Oracle. 'You will not be able to progress effectively if that is the case. So please become far more aware of what state you are in at any given moment of the day and return yourself far more frequently back to a state of rest by taking a moment to pause, taking a few deep breaths, and reminding yourself that there is no need to be fearful or anxious.'

This is indeed a more complicated step than I had initially imagined, I thought to myself. I made a mental note to myself to make sure I came back to this step at the end of the evening to reconfirm my understanding.

Returning to the whiteboard, The Oracle added another box below the ones he had drawn previously into which he wrote: Step 4: I rest knowing what I seek is already mine.

> **Step 1: I have committed to a divine and audacious intention**
> I am here to realize my full potential and help all those I come into contact with realize theirs. I will do this by: Loving and being loved. Doing my Great Work. Maintaining a healthy body and mind and reconnecting to the spirit. Securing my financial freedom. Enjoying the journey.

> **Step 2:**
> I have embraced a new set of limitless beliefs
> *The 12 Core Beliefs*

> **Step 3:**
> I act in alignment with my virtuous Code of Conduct
> *The A to Z of Life*

> **Step 4: I rest knowing what I seek is already mine**

He looked approvingly at the emerging diagram, then brought his attention back to the audience. 'I suspect you will now be sensing the need to fundamentally change the way you think about life,' said The Oracle.

'There is a need to improve our self-talk. The very common, *I am not good enough*, *I don't have enough*, needs to be replaced with the simple but powerful *I rest knowing what I seek is already mine.*

'Which is probably an opportune moment to clarify the greatest myth that pervades modern society. A revelation that has the potential to free you from all suffering and bring everlasting happiness. I have alluded to it already under step two, but just to ensure there is no confusion, let me take a moment to convey what I consider to be the greatest secret of all.'

Well that definitely sounds interesting, I thought to myself. *What could this revelation be?*

'You think it's normal to get upset, and feel stressed and anxious. But life isn't supposed to be that way. It's only because we are believing something that isn't true,' said The Oracle.

'But don't worry, you are not alone in this delusional thinking,' he added reassuringly. 'Of the billions of people on our planet, only a few have discovered the truth. And the truth is that you are not who you think you are! We have mistaken our identity; we are ignorant to our true nature.'

The real you is the spirit

'The *body* is what most people associate with and know best,' explained The Oracle. 'While it is the portal to everything we experience with our six senses – the things we can see, hear, touch, feel, taste and smell – it is not the real you. You are not your body.

'Nor are you your *mind* for that matter – that voice inside your head, the *thoughts* that direct the body, although the mind is the true creator of your physical reality, and it serves you well through its ability to clarify intention and focus attention. For example, moving your arm is an act of the mind.' The Oracle lifted his arm. 'Yet the mind is not the real you either.

'Your mind is an imposter pretending to be you. So, you don't need to work out which of your many and conflicting thoughts are the real you, because none of them are. You are not your thoughts.

'No! The real you is the one who hears those thoughts, the one who hears that voice talking. The real you is always silent. Observing. Aware. The witness. The real you is not even a human being. The real you is the *spirit*.

'Why's that important? Well, it's important to form that distinction and create that separation, because – despite its usefulness when properly managed – left in the driving seat, the mind can be a real troublemaker.

'When the mind is allowed to step beyond its useful function – something it will continually attempt to do – it will keep you imprisoned within a fabricated world, within a fabricated personality. You are and could be so much more than this.

'Being reunited with the spirit changes everything. It allows your heart to open, fear to dissipate, greed to diminish and happiness to grow.

'Thich Nhat Hanh, the Buddhist monk, said: "Enlightenment, for a wave in the ocean, is the moment it realizes it is water." Similarly, enlightenment for us humans is the moment we realize we are the spirit that fills the interspaces of the universe.

'Like a wave rising from the ocean, we hold a unique form for a period before we return to our origin. But we were always one with that origin, just as the wave is one with the ocean. The real you is not the wave but the ocean.

'To understand this is very powerful. Hopefully it's easy to see how a wave is not as big or as strong as the whole ocean. In a similar fashion I hope it's now dawning on you how much power you rob yourself of when you also imagine yourself as separate to the whole, separate to the spirit.

'To suggest that the wave and the ocean are not one and the same, that they are independent, is wrong. To suggest that the many—' The Oracle swept his hand across the room '—are not part of the one is equally wrong.

'We are no more independent of the spirit than the wave is of the ocean. If you attempt to take the wave away from the ocean, away from its source, it lacks the power of the ocean. That is what so many people have done with their life. This lost connection, this apparent duality, is not only a delusion but the root cause of your diminished power and nearly all human suffering.

'Once this truth becomes apparent, you can never live an *ordinary* life again. Once this connection is made, you will discover that we are not only more than we imagined, but more than we can imagine. We are boundless and expansive.

Ouch, I thought to myself. I could see how easy it would be to fall into this trap. I could see why this was being called the greatest secret of all. I suspect I had convinced myself that I was a wave yet in reality I was really the ocean.

'You only appear to be small and limited,' said The Oracle, 'because that's the version of yourself that you are focusing on. In reality, you are divinity in disguise. The real you is a genius, and paradoxically the closer you are to the real you – while living – the greater will be your ability to manipulate material reality, and the more at ease you will feel about life. You will achieve far more with less effort.

'For most of the population, however – and this really bothers me,' said The Oracle, with startling gravity, 'this realization, this a-ha moment, only happens at the very end of life – the very end, as in the moment you take your last breath.

'Now, this is one of life's greatest tragedies,' insisted The Oracle. 'The fact that most people only arrive at the real starting point of life when it's all over is crazy.' The Oracle shook his head. 'What a terrible waste.

'But, thankfully, that will not be your destiny. This will not be the plight of those assembled here tonight because you now know better.' He looked around the room lovingly, as a shepherd might gaze upon his flock. 'If I can achieve anything here tonight, let it be to save you from that fate.'

Wow, that is very different to the way I have always thought of myself, I reflected. I agreed that could change everything.

The Oracle rose to his feet and held his hands out wide as if to embrace the room. 'Keep in mind, however, that transcendence or reconnecting with your true self is not the destination; it's the *starting point.* So, please do all you can to get there *now.*'

'How do we get there?' came the question from the crowd.

'Brilliant,' shot back The Oracle without hesitation, 'I love the enthusiasm. Beyond what I have just outlined, what you ask is a perfect segue into the next five steps in our process where we will answer that question more fully.

'Shall I go on?'

The open and willing faces were all he needed to continue.

Step Five

I HAVE IMMERSED MYSELF IN THE SEVEN GREAT LOVE AFFAIRS

After a moment or two of silence, The Oracle let out a great 'Ahhhhh … ,' with plenty of emotion and an element of theatrics. 'Now we turn to my favorite topic. Love!

'Let me begin by repeating something the great Viktor Frankl once said:

For the first time in my life I saw the truth as it is set into song by so many poets, proclaimed as the final wisdom by so many thinkers. The truth – that love is the ultimate and highest goal to which man can aspire. Then I grasped the meaning of the greatest secret that human poetry and human thought and belief have to impart: The salvation of man is through love and in love.

He stopped, caught in a moment of deep reflection. 'Such beautiful words, don't you think?' he said, raising his head so he could hold us in his gaze. 'Now, it's up to you to make them a reality. He calls it the greatest secret. Well, let's not keep it a secret any longer,' he said, chuckling to himself. 'This should be the world's greatest known truth.'

The seven great love affairs

'See to it that you become the world's greatest lover,' he now said squarely to a young man seated near the front of the room, who turned a dark shade of red at the suggestion, 'and embark on seven truly great love affairs.'

'That's right,' he continued, mercifully averting his focus from the young man back to the room more generally. 'Embark on *seven* great love affairs and I promise you the outcome will not be nearly as exhausting as you might imagine; in fact, the opposite is true. The task will be truly invigorating.

'And who will benefit from all this loving?' The Oracle said cheekily. 'That's simple ...

'First of all, *you*. I want you to love yourself, for you cannot give to others what you do not have. Nor can you reach out to others for the love that you are not giving yourself. Nor can we live happily and freely if we run away from our own darkness.

'Second, your partner. I want you to love your partner, share their excitement and support them in the creation of their own happiness, as together you can double the joy and halve the sorrow of life.

'Third, your children. Love your children should you have them, for they are the sons and daughters of life's longing for itself.

'Next, your friends and family. Love your friends and family because, together, you can achieve anything.

'Fifth, all others. That's my *catch all* clause,' he said jokingly. 'But seriously, love all others without exception and without condition – every other living creature on this fair earth, and, in doing so, experience firsthand their divine core and essence. If each of us were to love those all around us, we could bring peace and harmony to the world.

'Next, love the planet. That on which you rely upon for so much, for what befalls the earth, befalls us all.

'And, finally, love all that you do. I implore you to love all that you do – the good, the bad and the ugly. The small and the mundane.

'And, don't be daunted by this task,' The Oracle added with conviction. 'You have a great capacity to love, an endless capacity to love. Love is not a scarce resource; you have an unlimited supply to give.

'Each and every one of these seven love affairs not only demands your attention but will make the world a far better place.'

I wrote them down as a series of dot points ...

- Love yourself
- Love your partner
- Love your children
- Love your friends and family
- Love all others without exception
- Love the planet
- Love all that you do.

It certainly seemed like an important list. But also, a bit overwhelming. I would like to think I was up to the task, but only time would tell. I could see it would be worth the effort, however.

Before we could move on, a hand went up near the back of the room. 'Questions!' said The Oracle. 'Great, I welcome questions!' He pointed to the woman in the crowd.

'Can you tell us more about loving ourselves?' she asked. 'You mention it as the first great love affair, but I suspect I speak on behalf of most people here when I say it doesn't come easily.'

'You're right,' agreed The Oracle. 'I'm with you. Based on my own experience and the experience of those I have come across, this is definitely something we don't do very well.

'What is it then that makes it such a hard task to master?' The Oracle said inquiringly.

'Well, the answer lies in our shadow, I believe, and the difficulty we find in facing ourselves with honesty.

'Most of us have locked up enormous amounts of energy in a submerged part of our personality called "the shadow". This is where we try to hide our faults, flaws and aspects of ourselves that we don't like. But trying to hide our shadow is like trying to hold a beach ball under water. It's difficult and exhausting!' The Oracle mimicked the act, drawing a few chuckles from the audience.

I immediately connected with what he was saying, yet I had no idea what the solution was.

'The charade we are living when we do this destroys our relationships, kills our spirit, keeps us from fulfilling our dreams and restricts our ability to achieve true and lasting success.

'The solution? Well, you need to stop concealing what it is you cannot accept about yourself.

'You need to focus on being whole, rather than good. You need to lead an integrated life. Instead of trying to suppress your shadow, you need to own and embrace the things you are most afraid of facing. Doing so will free you to experience your magnificent whole for the first time since early childhood. The good, the bad and the ugly. The parts of you that you have suppressed are desperate to be reintegrated.

'Own the fact that you can have bad thoughts, that you have moments of envy, moments of hatred. The thoughts are natural and not the problem. It's only if you act on them that the problem starts. Thoughts and actions are not the same thing. Be very selective in what you act on, but don't deny the existence of your negative qualities.

'Ironically, these suppressed qualities are only really harmful when they remain suppressed. Once you honor their existence – once they are embraced and reunited – you can choose the contribution they make to your life.

'How many of you were raised to believe you should hide certain things about yourself to be accepted by others?' Most people in the audience raised their hands.

'Exactly! Most of us were taught that people have good traits and bad traits, and that we should get rid of, or hide, the bad. However, the reality is quite different. We cannot get rid of one thing without also denying its opposite. Good and bad, greed and gratitude, night and day – these are different sides of the same coin. Hide bad and you also hide good. You cannot have one without the other.

'They're all part of the balanced world in which we live. There is nothing we can see or conceive that we are not. Fear, anger, envy, sorrow – all of these are part of us and will act out if they are not recognized as an integral part of our psyche.

'Recognizing that it's normal to possess these less-desirable qualities is an important step in our self-awareness and our evolution to being whole once again.

'And that's the objective. Being whole.'

The room remained silent as we reflected on what had been said, and then another question was asked.

'You talk about no longer suppressing all our negative qualities, but isn't that risky?' asked a stern-sounding man just behind me. 'Wouldn't that result in chaos if we all did it?'

'Not at all. And here's why,' responded The Oracle. 'Good and evil will always coexist. This is part of the balanced world in which we live, but we can control the negative.

'In this instance, I am reminded of the village elder, as he sat around the campfire one evening with his grandchildren.

'"There is a fight going on inside me each day between two wolves," he said. "A black wolf and a white wolf. The black wolf represents fear, anger, envy, sorrow, regret, greed, arrogance, self-pity, guilt, resentment, inferiority, lies, false pride, superiority and ego. The white wolf stands for joy, peace, love, hope, sharing, serenity, humility, kindness, benevolence, friendship, empathy, generosity, truth, compassion and faith. This same fight is going on inside you and inside every other person."

'His grandchildren thought about it for a minute, then one child asked his grandfather: "Which wolf will win?"

'The old man simply replied, "The one you feed."

'Take comfort knowing you have the ability to use the negative qualities sparingly, if at all,' said The Oracle, as his eyes lit up. 'Although they remain part of us, they need not play a role in our life. See yourselves as peaceful warriors who rise to the peaceful challenge each and every day to feed the white wolf and starve the black wolf.'

It surprised me that The Oracle was condoning negative emotions, especially when he was someone who approached life with such a positive, optimistic outlook. Negative emotions such as anger and resentment had been recurring themes for me in my adolescence, which I wasn't proud of. To now recognize the need for their existence, and the potential to acknowledge their occurrence as normal but know that despite their occurrence I did not have to act on them, was refreshing to hear. I could see how I could use this approach to improve my life from this point onwards. *This is definitely something I want to put into action more fully*, I thought.

The Oracle added this step five to the Life Plan.

> **Step 1: I have committed to a divine and audacious intention**
> I am here to realize my full potential and help all those I come into contact with realize theirs. I will do this by: Loving and being loved. Doing my Great Work. Maintaining a healthy body and mind and reconnecting to the spirit. Securing my financial freedom. Enjoying the journey.

> **Step 2:**
> I have embraced a new set of limitless beliefs
> *The 12 Core Beliefs*

> **Step 3:**
> I act in alignment with my virtuous Code of Conduct
> *The A to Z of Life*

> **Step 4: I rest knowing what I seek is already mine**

> **Step 5: I have immersed myself in the seven great love affairs**

'Well done,' he said, turning to face us. 'You are now more than halfway there. Hopefully you are still with me?'

I suspected we were, as I hadn't seen a single person leave.

Step Six

I AM DOING MY GREAT WORK

'Now before we go further,' began The Oracle, 'I should clarify that we have now entered the *doing* part of our system.

'To put that into context, let me explain one of my favorite abbreviations regarding life,' said The Oracle.

'If someone ever asked me to briefly impart what I had learnt about life, I would utter these three simple words: Be, Do, Have. Or more precisely Have, Be, Do.' I wrote them down as it sounded simple, but I had never heard this expression before.

$$Have - Be - Do$$

The Oracle went on to explain further. 'The HAVE is about defining your audacious goals. Our step one. The BE is where the magic lies, the all-important *beliefs* and *behaviors* and *being* that make everything possible. Our steps two, three and four. The DO is about taking the necessary action to make these audacious goals a reality. Our remaining four steps, including the previous step five, are all about the *doing*.

'Having spent the first half of my life delivering large, complex projects, I know quite a lot about the *doing* side of things,' shared The Oracle. 'And, while there always appeared to be so many issues in need of attention, in the end, success would always boil down to two key factors: are we doing the right things, and are we doing those things right?

'The challenge in our own life is no different. If we do the right things, and we do those things right, we will get to live a remarkable life.' The Oracle drew a simple four-box matrix on the whiteboard, into which he wrote the words Remarkable Life, Lost Opportunity, Ordinary Life and Plodder.

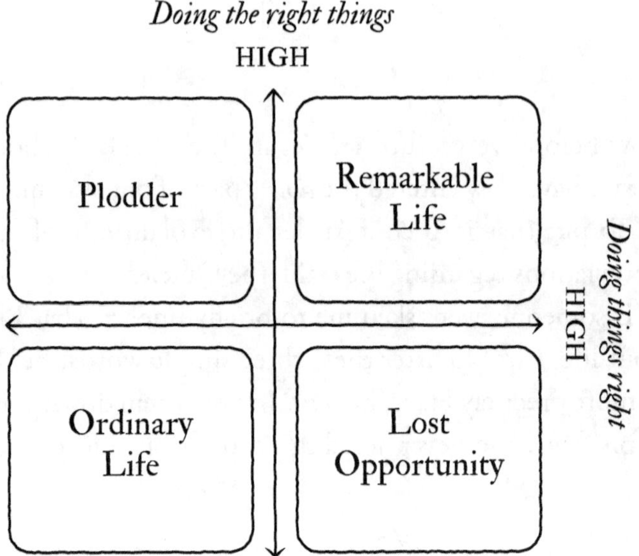

'If we do the right things, but don't do them right, on the other hand, you become what I call a *plodder*,' he said, pointing to the top-left quadrant. 'In that realm you have noble intentions, but they never materialize because you didn't do those things right.

'Equally, if you do things really well, but you're not doing the right things, then – although there is plenty of progression – it doesn't take you to where you need to be. You do a great job climbing the ladder, only to find when you get to the top that you had it leaning against the wrong wall. That's what I call a *lost opportunity*,' he said, pointing to the bottom-right quadrant.

'And, finally, to complete the picture, if you neither do the right things, nor do them right, you will have an *ordinary* life. As the vast majority of the population do.

'You don't want to be *ordinary*; you don't want to be a *plodder* and you certainly don't want your life to be a *lost opportunity*,' advised The Oracle. 'My job is to ensure you are one of the few who lives a **remarkable life**.

'We have just covered what that means you must do in terms of Love, let's now turn our attention to what that means you need to do, and do right, in terms of your Great Work. What better place to practice the art of doing than doing the work that you were born to do?!'

Your gift to the world

The Oracle took a moment to compose himself and take a sip of water before continuing.

'Step six is all about your Great Work. See this as your gift to the world. What you will exchange for your success.'

I had never thought of work that way before, but I really liked the idea of a fair exchange. I give you something of significant value and you deliver me success in return.

'The world needs improvement in every form of human endeavor, so please don't wait for others to do what's required,' said The Oracle. 'Bring forth your great deeds no matter what your field of endeavor or level of experience, so we can all benefit.

'As for what that Great Work might be – well, my experience suggests your Great Work will lie at the intersection of seven things.'

The Oracle got to his feet and drew a large circle, in which he wrote 'Great Work', then drew a further seven circles around it, and added some arrows connecting them ...

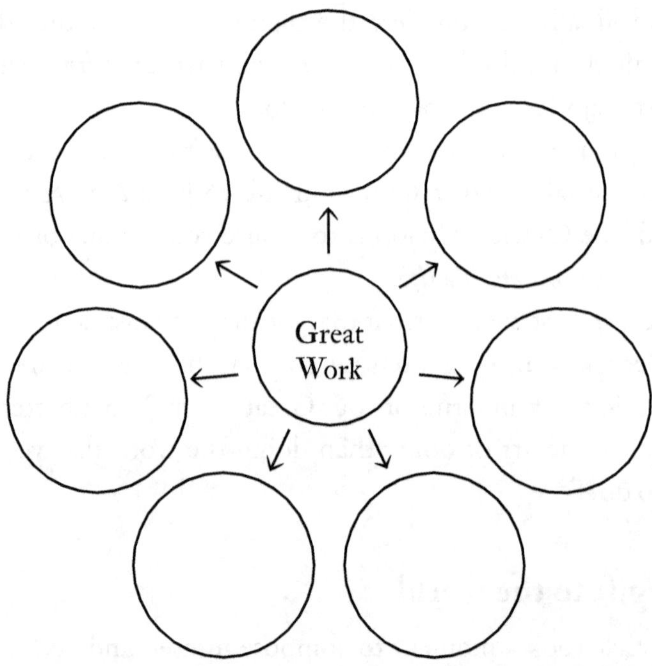

For your Great Work to be truly great, ideally it will satisfy the following seven criteria,' said The Oracle.

- 'Firstly, **Love:** It's important to love what you do. Note this is different to doing what you love. There are many things you can genuinely learn to love doing. The simple test here is, do you lose track of time when you are doing it?

- 'Secondly, **Unique:** Is what you do or what you provide unique, or can you do it uniquely well? The world doesn't need more of the same.

- 'Thirdly, **Highly Valued:** Will the world really value what you have to offer? Would they mourn its loss if it were no longer available?

'Combine this with the above and you're onto a real winner: something that is both unique and highly valued.

- 'Fourthly, **Viable:** Can you make reasonable money doing it? This is the airplane oxygen mask theory at play. Clearly you need to be able to look after yourself before you can begin to look after others.

- 'Fifthly, **Growth:** Does it provide you the ongoing opportunity for growth and development?

- 'Sixthly, **Enjoyable:** Can you do it with great people in a great place? Don't just pass over this criteria either. Although it may at first feel less important than the others, you really won't be satisfied for long if you are forced to work in a location you do not enjoy or with people you do not respect and like.

- 'Finally, **Responsible:** Is it environmentally and socially responsible? That is to say, it will not harm the planet or others on the planet.

'Now, this is a really empowering concept to grasp,' said The Oracle, pausing to write each of these points in their own circles.

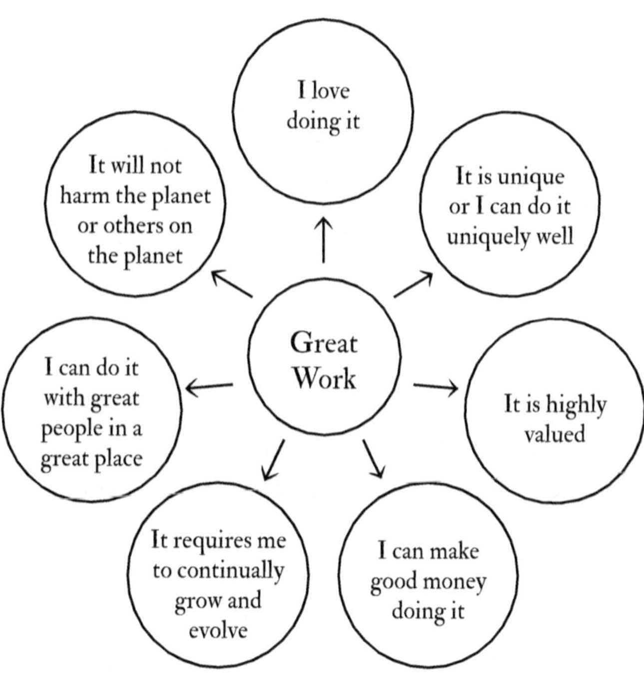

'Get these seven things in place and you will have the opportunity to become famous. Famous at least to those you serve, who will praise the day you were born and be forever thankful for the positive impact your product or service has had on their life.

'What could be more rewarding than that?'

The Oracle added this step to the Life Plan.

Step 1: I have committed to a divine and audacious intention
I am here to realize my full potential and help all those I come into contact with realize theirs. I will do this by: Loving and being loved. Doing my Great Work. Maintaining a healthy body and mind and reconnecting to the spirit. Securing my financial freedom. Enjoying the journey.

Step 2:
I have embraced a new set of limitless beliefs
The 12 Core Beliefs

Step 3:
I act in alignment with my virtuous Code of Conduct
The A to Z of Life

Step 4: I rest knowing what I seek is already mine

Step 5: I have immersed myself in the seven great love affairs

Step 6: I am doing my Great Work

'You can create something that doesn't already exist,' said The Oracle. 'Or you can do something others already do but do it better. Either way, the opportunities for Great Work are numerous,' he said.

'And don't be easily put off by the need to make reasonable money doing it. Given the global marketplace you can now so easily access, I would be surprised if you can't make a decent living doing whatever you might have in mind.

'But do be careful – I hear people say: "just do what you love". Don't fall for this dangerous oversimplification because, you know what? It's not all about you! Your success will be driven by the extent to which you create success for others, not the other way around.

'Whether you are operating in the private sector or the not-for-profit sector, whether you are a parent raising a child with love, an aid worker helping to transform the lives of the less fortunate or an entrepreneur launching your latest product, Great Work is all about service to others or, more specifically, providing a highly valued product or service to a large and thirsty crowd.

'A good business can have a good impact on the world by doing something that matters a good deal to a good number of people. A great business can have a great impact on the world by doing something that matters a great deal to a great number of people. A remarkable business can have a remarkable impact on the world by doing something that makes a remarkable difference to the lives of a remarkable number of people.

'The more lives you impact, directly or indirectly, the more value you will create. Love what you do by all means, this is critical, but make sure it's also something the world really wants or needs. That's the real secret to Great Work: what you can do for others.

'If there is something you really love doing but others don't want it, find something else to do that satisfies both criteria. There are plenty of things you can end up loving. You can still do the other thing you love on the side, but it becomes your hobby, not your Great Work. Great Work lies at the intersection of all seven criteria.

'This step six is all about service,' said The Oracle by way of summary. 'Helping others to achieve their goals in life. Do this well and you will be richly rewarded.'

Step Seven

I PRACTICE THE TEN STEPS OF PERFECT HEALTH AND TRANSCENDENCE

The Oracle closed his eyes and composed himself, taking three deep breaths, inhaling slowly and then exhaling in a similarly measured fashion. Nothing had changed – he remained seated on the stool facing us and we sat attentively facing him – yet the moment felt inexplicably new, and what might follow full of renewed promise.

As he opened his eyes and looked at us, there was an unfathomable warmth in his expression. A gentle radiating glow that could melt a frozen landscape.

'Hmmmmmm,' he said, more in the manner of a chant than an attempt to communicate. 'Where to begin?'

Although it was floated as a question, the room had no need to answer. We all knew The Oracle would know exactly where to begin and we sensed the importance of what was about to follow.

Harmonious, enlightened beings

'You can think of yourself as being made up of three parts,' he finally offered, 'the body, mind and spirit. Each one plays a crucial role in facilitating a joyous, healthy and enlightened earthly experience.

'When we are all mind, things become far too structured and mechanical. When we are all spirit, things can get far too fluid to navigate successfully in this rather structured world. When we are all body, things become far too superficial. But when all three work together, we can become harmonious, enlightened beings.

'Contrary to popular opinion, far from decaying, the body and the brain are a cohesive engine of evolution. Within each of us is a healing system that ensures all functions of the body are perfectly performed. It can renew us when we are worn out, eliminate waste and poisonous matter, and repair us when we are broken. You are meant to be free of pain and have abundant energy. Abundant health is available to anyone. Assuming, that is—' The Oracle halted to make sure he had everyone's attention '—you do three things:

- 'First, you need to *think well*. Imperfect thoughts will cause imperfect functioning, which in turn causes our bodies dis-ease, and ultimately disease. A daily "diet" of negative low-vibrational thoughts is no different to consuming junk food. So, think of yourself as being perfectly well, enjoying a perfectly strong and healthy body that is full of life and vitality. Imagine yourself doing your work easily and with no end of stamina, never feeling tired or weak. Know that your body will continually rebuild itself with perfectly healthy cells. That all of its internal functioning will be performed in a perfectly healthy manner. Rest assured that there is far more health power than disease power in both you and in the environment. Rejoice in the knowledge that you live, move and exist in a limitless ocean of health, where age doesn't count. We have touched on this already as one of our core beliefs under step two, so I won't go on.

- 'Second, if a person thinks well but does not support that mindset by living in a healthy manner, then these actions will cause their bodies to become diseased. So, you will need to support your thinking with a healthy lifestyle by doing things like eating well, moving well, breathing well, and getting plenty of sleep.

- 'Thirdly, and in my opinion most importantly, you need to reconnect with the spirit, the real you, and then stay connected throughout the day through the practice of mindfulness.

'Expanding on this a little further then,' said The Oracle, holding up his ten fingers, 'and assuming that we already have the first step of *thinking well* covered elsewhere, our ten steps to perfect health are as follows:

1. '*Eat and drink well:* watch what you eat and drink, when you eat, and how you eat.

2. '*Move well:* the body is designed to move. It needs regular exercise to maintain fitness, bone density and muscle bulk, prevent weight gain, reduce stress, boost energy levels, and generally enable you to live a healthier and more active life.

3. '*Sleep well:* every living thing needs sleep. Even plants have resting periods. When we sleep, our lives are renewed with vital energy and given new strength. It is of fundamental importance that we sleep in a natural and healthy manner.

4. '*Breathe well:* breathe through the nose, not through the mouth. The body relies on the nose's ability to pressurize, filter, and heat up the air before it enters the lungs. Inhale deeply, expanding the diaphragm. Exhale more fully so that you can in turn take in more fresh air. Breathe less and more slowly. The perfect breath is to inhale for 5.5 seconds and then exhale for 5.5 seconds.'

The Oracle demonstrated just such a breath before continuing.

5. '*Release any trapped negative emotions:* we all suffer from a raft of suppressed emotions like fear, anger, disgust, jealousy, and envy that separate us from our divine nature, limit our health

and access to energy, and so prevent us from realizing our full potential. Let your emotional weather pass through you.

6. '*Heal yourself of unprocessed trauma by reframing the past:* we have all suffered trauma. It is the root cause of most suffering. But there is no need to be a prisoner of the past. Turn your scars into trophies. We are our greatest healers. When you heal yourself, you heal the world.

7. '*Move away from that which causes you unhealthy dis-ease and toward relief:* while it is good to be challenged and stretched, where the dis-ease we are feeling is ongoing and unhealthy, it will soon translate into some form of chronic disease.

8. '*Don't expose yourself to toxins:* remove them from your home, your workplace and where necessary your body. Common culprits include cleaning chemicals, herbicides, pesticides, some cosmetics and deodorants, smoking, drugs, food containers, and PCBs found in paints and certain plastics. And for the older members of the audience: mercury fillings. Your body is an important vehicle for you to journey through life; you need to respect it and care for it.

9. '*Rest and re-energize and reconnect with nature:* interestingly, stressful events are typically not the problem, it's the lack of recovery time between stressful events that ultimately takes its toll on our health. It is important therefore that you stop and re-energize yourself regularly to varying degrees. Take a micro refresh in the middle of a stressful task, an hour to relax at the end of a stressful day, a couple of days each week to recharge yourself and several weeks each year to revitalize. As much as possible reconnect with nature. Its regenerative benefits are well documented. The earth of our ancestors, the sea of our origin and the sunlight that sustains us are powerful and important allies in our life. You need to take care of yourself so you can take care of others.

10. '*Finally, reconnect with your true self via meditation, and then stay connected throughout the day by practicing mindfulness:* this is of course the most important and transformative step of all.

'These are the ten steps to perfect health and transcendence. While we will not have time to go into detail on each of these here tonight, these steps are eminently doable and much has already been written on each if you require further direction.

'Let me capture this important step in our Life Plan for future reference,' said The Oracle, adding a new box in which he wrote the words: Step 7: I practice the 10 steps of perfect health and transcendence.

Step 1: I have committed to a divine and audacious intention
I am here to realize my full potential and help all those I come into contact with realize theirs. I will do this by: Loving and being loved. Doing my Great Work. Maintaining a healthy body and mind and reconnecting to the spirit. Securing my financial freedom. Enjoying the journey.

Step 2:
I have embraced a new set of limitless beliefs
The 12 Core Beliefs

Step 3:
I act in alignment with my virtuous Code of Conduct
The A to Z of Life

Step 4: I rest knowing what I seek is already mine

Step 5: I have immersed myself in the seven great love affairs

Step 6: I am doing my Great Work

Step 7: I practice the 10 steps of perfect health and transcendence

As I looked over his list, I was painfully aware of the opportunity for further improvement in my own life. Breathing was something I had certainly never focused on, and I suspect there was also some healing of past trauma to be done. It was probably also time to finally have another go at meditation. There were just too many people singing its praises to ignore any longer. *Note to future self!* I thought, as my attention was brought back to the room by a question.

Releasing trapped emotions

'What about *releasing trapped emotions*?' enquired a young woman reading from her notes. 'You mentioned it is a key step in achieving perfect health, and I'm sensing it's important, but it's not something I would know how to do.'

'Brilliant,' said The Oracle. 'I agree, this is a critical process that is not at all well understood, so it definitely warrants further discussion.

'Think of it as emotional indigestion. We have this nasty habit of turning difficult or painful moments into lasting pain and ultimately disease simply because we have not learnt to let go.

'You see, everything in the universe is made of energy, and emotions are no exception. They are simply vibrating pure energy with their own unique frequency. When these emotions are released into our bodies, which are also pure vibrating energy, this new energy affects our existing energy in either a positive or negative way. This is why emotions can affect us on both an emotional and physical level.

'Disease is caused by an energy imbalance in the body, and much of our disease is due to negative emotional energies that have become trapped within us. If our objective is perfect health, then we need to let go of negative emotions such as anger and resentment, releasing all that energy so it is available to us in day-to-day life.

'The sources of these trapped negative emotions can be numerous. Relationship problems, breakdown, financial hardship, feelings of inferiority, work stress, loss of loved ones, miscarriage, abortion, negative self-talk, physical trauma, rejection, physical, mental, verbal or sexual abuse – the list is long.' The Oracle paused as if to honor any trauma we might feel.

'To make matters even worse, while most of these blocked emotions are a direct result of our own life experiences, some can also be inherited from the lives and hardships of our ancestors. Though we once thought the slate was wiped clean from generation to generation, there is now evidence that trauma can be carried across generations.

'For example,' said The Oracle, 'the neuroscientists at Emory University, in the US, taught mice to fear the smell of cherry blossoms by associating the scent with mild electric shocks. The offspring of these mice were then raised to adulthood having never been exposed to this smell, yet when they were exposed to it for the first time they suddenly became anxious and fearful.

'Unfortunately, time does not necessarily heal all wounds.

'So, what to do? Well, keep in mind that emotions per se are not the problem here. They play an important role in our daily life and should therefore not be shunned. They are vital to our survival. The issue is purely those emotions that are trapped within us, because we have either suppressed them in an attempt to disconnect from our pain or given them unnecessary attention to the point we are now dominated by our pain.

'But don't lose heart ... it is not a hard problem to fix. It's just that none of us have ever really been taught what to do. I know I wasn't until very recently,' he said, looking a little sheepish.

Dealing with difficult emotions

'What I would recommend is a four-step process when an experience or event gives rise to a strong negative emotional response.

- 'First, observe the presence of that negative emotion with interest, as a somewhat detached witness might do. As if you were watching yourself like a movie from a distance.

- 'Second, welcome that emotion, no matter how painful or uncomfortable it may be. Lean into it rather than pulling away from it. We can't heal what is ignored. Remain open and vulnerable rather than closing down. Hold it, breathe with it, relax with it and just say, *Okay, I accept you. I'm not running from you.*

- 'Third, if it is a particularly strong emotion then write your thoughts down on paper and confide in someone close to you, to assist you in making sense of what is going on in your mind. This step will help to ensure that you understand and can verbalize what it is that is making you feel as you do. Talking openly will mean these negative emotions are less likely to become suppressed.

- 'And finally, when you are ready, let the emotion pass through you and move on.

'That's it!

'While this process might cause you discomfort in the short term, it will ensure you do no long-term damage to your health. Our tendency is to push painful thoughts away, but know that any attempt to avoid legitimate suffering lies at the root of emotional-related illness and disease.

'Problems start when any of these four steps are interrupted, and the emotional experience is left incomplete.

'If instead of embracing an emotion we attempt to resist or reject it because it's causing us pain, it will become trapped. Ironically, these negative emotions can cause us damage only if we attempt to deny them. What we resist will persist.

'Likewise, if we hold onto it and do not let it pass through us, then the trapped energy of that negative emotion will cause a disturbance in our body's energy field. The more overwhelming or extreme an emotion is, the more likely it is to become trapped.

'Consciously clear away any of this baggage to become who you really are. Otherwise, both your present and your future will be held hostage by your past.

'When you have cleaned up the past, the trick is to stop the accumulation of the new.

'Does that adequately answer your question?' asked The Oracle.

'Perfect, thank you,' was the response from the woman.

'Excellent, then unless there are any more questions, let's move on,' said The Oracle. We all remained silent. 'Right then,' he said, clearly excited by the opportunity to continue. 'I love this next step,' he said, slapping his knees, 'I hope you will too.'

Step Eight

I HAVE SECURED MY FINANCIAL FREEDOM BY IMPLEMENTING THE SEVEN LAWS

'Step eight is all about freedom,' began The Oracle. 'Given every-one here tonight already enjoys the basic freedoms of speech, religion, sexual orientation, political persuasion, assembly, and others, our focus here and now is on your financial freedom. Or more precisely, the accumulation of sufficient money to be able to do what you want, when you want.

'Now this is something I actually did quite well from a rela-tively young age,' said The Oracle, 'so I am fortunate to now have the resources I require at my disposal to travel around the world and hold forums such as this, helping others to enrich their lives.

'And by the way,' added The Oracle with some eagerness, 'the sooner you start the better. Time makes a profound difference here. It really, really does, as you are about to discover.'

I'm glad we've got to this, I thought to myself. I could certainly do with some help in this area. Yet there were others in the room who clearly felt differently ...

'Can I say,' came a voice from the audience, 'that I am a little surprised by the importance being placed on money, and wonder whether it really belongs in the same realm as what is being discussed here tonight. Isn't it being overly materialistic to include it as one of the key intentions?'

'I understand your reservation, madam,' responded The Oracle, 'for the relationship between money and happiness is indeed a controversial one. Clearly, money cannot buy happiness, but give me a chance to explain how a measured amount can certainly help you live a remarkable life and hopefully convince you of the reason for its inclusion.

'By the way, I am not advocating financial excess here, folks,' cautioned The Oracle, 'but a certain amount of money has been repeatedly shown to increase a family's overall level of happiness. A phenomenon well expressed in a typical bell curve such as this.' The Oracle got to his feet and drew a sweeping arc on the whiteboard.

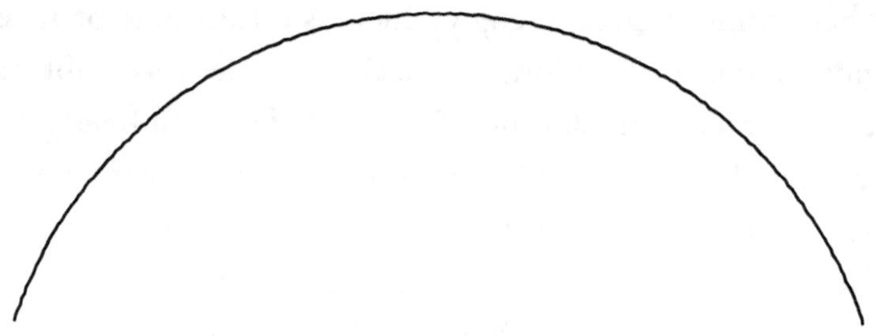

'We need to attain a certain level of wealth or financial independence to meet our basic needs – the ability to provide food, clothing, shelter, and so on.'

To the arc he added an X-axis, labeling it 'Money spent', and a Y-axis, which he labeled 'Fulfillment'. He then placed the words Survival, Comforts and Luxuries along the curve, and above Luxuries he wrote the word ENOUGH.

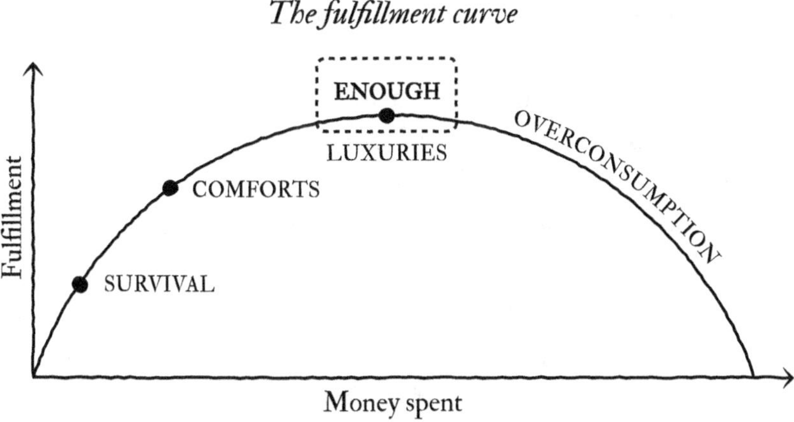

Pointing at the bottom left of the curve, he went on to explain …

'When you have barely enough money to live, yet those around you are enjoying a comfortable life, you will typically be miserable. You will feel like you are in survival mode,' he said, tapping the word *survival* with his finger, 'living from paycheck to paycheck, struggling to make ends meet.

'If you find a way to increase your income and move beyond mere survival to achieve a more comfortable life, then your level of happiness will typically increase in a commensurate manner.

'If you were to continue that path and move from being merely comfortable to a place where you gain access to a few more of life's little luxuries, then your level of happiness is likely to peak.' The Oracle pointed to the top of the curve. 'Interestingly, beyond that point, the level of happiness typically starts to decline as income further increases.

'So, what do we take from this? Well, if the money you currently have at your disposal places you to the left of our midpoint, then increasing your wealth is likely to have a positive impact on your happiness. But increasing your wealth beyond that point will make you richer, but not typically happier.

'I say *typically*, because by following the path we are laying out here tonight, I believe you can acquire any amount of wealth and still be happy, understanding that money in itself is not evil. But I'm getting a little sidetracked. To keep things simple for now, are we in agreement that the accumulation of some wealth – what we might describe as securing your financial freedom – is an extremely valid goal in our pursuit of happiness?'

The room was silent. I looked around. Most people appeared to be nodding.

'Madam, you initially raised some concern at the inclusion of this step,' said The Oracle, directly addressing the woman who had initially voiced her concerns. 'How do you feel now after that brief justification? Are you happy if I go on?'

'Yes, that was very helpful thank you, and hard to dispute. Please go on,' she said.

'Excellent. *How then do we achieve such an outcome?* is the obvious next question,' said The Oracle, tilting his head toward us.

The Seven Laws of Financial Freedom

'Well, in essence, you need to do seven things, which we call our Seven Laws of Financial Freedom – and they are as follows ...

'Law 1: Set up five bank accounts and automatically allocate money to them

'*Account # 1* is your *emergency fund*. Into this you should allocate a minimum of 10% – and ideally up to 20% – of everything you earn. Initially this will be used to pay down any bad debt, and once that is dealt with you should allow it to accumulate until you have sufficient money in it to allow you to live for six months if you suddenly lost your job and had no income. That's why we call this your emergency fund. It provides a very important financial buffer.

'*Account # 2* is your *new car* account. For many people this is the largest single purchase they need to make, thus it is helpful to plan ahead. So, if you do need a car in your life, you should place into this account an amount each month that is sufficient to replace your vehicle, or vehicles, every 10 years. If for instance I believe I need $30,000 to purchase a new car every 10 years, then I would automatically allocate $250 per month into this account ($250 × 12 × 10 = $30,000).

'*Account # 3* is your *everyday* account. This the regular day-to-day account into which your salary is paid, and all your living expenses are paid out of. This is the account you should have your debit card linked to – if you have one.

'*Account # 4* is what I call your *vagabonding* account. This is what you use to travel and splurge on yourself every so often. It should be linked to your everyday account so you can easily transfer into it any excess money you may have from time to time.

'*Account # 5* is your *investment* account. This is the most important account of all. This will become the foundation of your financial freedom. Once Account # 1 has been used to pay off any bad debt and it has reached its target *emergency* balance, those funds – a minimum of 10% but ideally 20% of everything you earn – should then be redirected into this account.

'Finally, pay very careful attention to the automation aspect of this step. You need to be automatically allocating money to these accounts,' emphasized The Oracle. 'It is crucial that you take the day-to-day decision out of your hands. You want this to happen by itself in the background with no effort on your part.'

'Law 2: Eliminate any bad debt and never expose yourself to it again

'Law 2 requires you to eliminate any *bad* debt you may have accumulated prior to embarking on this journey. What's the difference between good debt and bad debt? Well, good debt is used to fund the purchase of *appreciating* assets – things like real estate – that increase in value over time. This type of debt helps us to achieve our financial goals. Bad debt on the other hand becomes a growing burden from which it is hard to emerge victorious. Bad debt is used to purchase *depreciating* things like furniture, cars, boats, holidays and clothes. Bad debt acts like a parasite, attaching itself to you. For a period of time it may appear to enhance your life but, over time, as it grows in size, it will increasingly dominate you, robbing you of vital nutrients and light, until eventually you are totally overcome and die – financially that is – as well as emotionally. Nobody wants that to happen, so you need to act now and rid yourself of the parasite of bad debt in your life. To do so, you need to take the 10% to 20% you are allocating into Account #1 as a consequence of Law 1 above and use those funds to progressively and diligently eliminate bad debt from your life as quickly as you possibly can. If you have no bad debt, then congratulations. Well done. That is a great achievement. You can move onto Law 3, which is where the real magic starts.

'Law 3: Start investing wisely and ensure you receive an attractive return on investment

'Unfortunately, you can't just be a good saver and get ahead financially these days. You also need to take the next step and become a good investor. I say unfortunately because I acknowledge it would be much easier if saving alone was the goal. Investing certainly does add a further complication, but it is worth it. Well and truly worth it. To illustrate just how important investing, as opposed to merely saving, is, imagine you save $10 a day and place it under your mattress for the next 20 years. After 20 years you will have accumulated $73,000. But if you invested these savings along the way achieving 15% long-term average compound growth, you would end up with just over $460,000 rather than the original amount of $73,000. That's a big difference. So, this Law 3 is a real a biggie, and will have a huge impact on the results you will be able to achieve. Fortunately, it can be automated, requiring very little fuss if you start early enough in life. So, take the savings from account # 5 and regularly invest them in quality assets like shares and property that are likely to appreciate in value over time. And a couple of don'ts: don't invest in things you are not familiar with, and don't pursue get-rich-quick schemes.

'Law 4: Continually increase your earning capacity

'Law 4 is a particularly interesting one. All the other laws can be largely automated, *set and forget* so to speak, whereas this one will require your ongoing focus. Yet, if it's any form of compensation, this law can really make a difference, so it makes sense to invest time in its attainment. Grow your salary at 5% a year and it will double on average every 14.4 years. Grow it at 10% a year and it will double on average every 7.2 years. I will explain the significant impact of this difference in more detail shortly.

'Law 5: Vagabond

'Be adventurous. Master the art of taking time off (six weeks to twelve weeks each year) on a regular basis from your normal life to discover and experience the world on your own terms. Meet cool people, in cool places, and do cool things. Travel, and truly immerse yourself in exotic locations, learning from each new culture how they do things differently and opening yourself up to changing your own life and way of doing things based on what you learn. There is so much we could and should be doing differently, and more than likely someone elsewhere is doing it better. I'm a big believer in the view that *the future has already arrived. It's just not evenly distributed yet.* I myself have traveled extensively and been fortunate enough to live in five different countries, each one changing me in some important way. And if travel is not your thing? Well then, use the money to do what you love, brings you joy and enlarges your perspective. Enrich your life with those funds, from your vagabond account. Assuming you have put the other laws in place, you deserve it.

'Law 6: Protect yourself from significant downside

'One of the keys to wealth preservation is the appropriate management of downside risk. It is very unlikely that every investment you make will be a winner. So, you will need to cut nonperforming investments quickly and allow your good performers to build. This is not an investment seminar so I won't go into the details of how to do that, but it's very important that you understand this concept. It is also important to ensure you have your emergency funds in place, as these provide an essential income buffer. Likewise, make sure assets such as real estate are properly and adequately insured and that you also have other appropriate insurance in place; for example, life, health and income protection. Finally, if entering into business or operating in a profession where you may find yourself subject to litigation, it will also be important to hold your investment assets in the right structure to ensure they are, to the extent possible, safe if you become the subject of litigation.

'Law 7: Once you have what you need, help the less fortunate

'It's important that you know when you have enough to live a quality life. At this point, rather than just continuing to expand your own lifestyle, it's worth turning your attention to helping others. Happiness is not found in seeking more, but enjoying less. So know when enough is enough. Allocate surplus earnings from the investment portfolio you have accumulated under Law 3 to quality charities, dedicated to helping others. Andrew Carnegie captured this sentiment beautifully when he said, "I will spend the first half of my life making money and the second half of my life giving it away to do the most good and the least harm". And never doubt what opportunity there is for doing good. Here the task is clear; the world needs affordable **food, water and clothing** for all. Affordable clean **energy, sanitation and shelter** for all. Access to quality, affordable and premium **healthcare and education. Political freedom and freedom of speech** for all. **Equal opportunity and justice** for all, regardless of age, sex, gender, culture or religion. We need to care for the **environment** (land, waters, animals and plants, the air we breathe). We must ensure people have access to good **jobs** and live in communities that engender **friendship**, a sense of **connection**, plus **peace** and personal **safety**. That's quite a list, and I'm guessing you could make quite a significant contribution to it yourself.

The three key accelerators

'By implementing these seven laws,' The Oracle suggested, 'your money will work for you in time rather than you always having to work for money, and you will help to make the world a better place. You could leave quite a legacy not only for your own family but all those you have helped. That's quite a liberating thought!'

I had to agree; I found the whole idea of gaining my financial freedom quite liberating, and the idea of being able to help others was both refreshing and exhilarating.

'The key accelerators in this process are threefold,' said The Oracle, holding up three fingers. 'Namely, the amount of money you save and invest, the return on investment that you achieve, and finally, the rate at which you grow your earnings.

The Three Accelerators:

1. *The amount of money you save and invest*

2. *The return on investment you achieve*

3. *The rate at which you grow your earnings*

'To put that into context, let's assume you start working at 25 years of age on a salary of $50,000 per annum. If you grew that salary at 5% per year, saved and invested 5% of everything you earned, and achieved an average 5% return per annum on that investment over your working life – what do you think you might accumulate at the end?

'Well, after 40 years, your investment nest egg will be worth some $700,000 at the age of 65. Now remember that number.

'If instead of this,' said The Oracle, with a wry smile on his face, 'you listened really carefully to what I just said, and became an expert at applying our seven laws, the first four in particular, and as a consequence you ...

'Grew your salary at 10% rather than 5% a year. Plus, you saved 10% of everything you earned rather than 5%, and you achieved an average 10% return on investment over that period rather than a 5% return ...

'Then ... taking all this into account, your investment nest egg would be worth $9 million at age 65, rather than the $700,000 mentioned previously.

'Make the increases 15% rather than 10% and the number becomes $80 million. At 20% the number becomes $600 million.'

I scribbled down the four numbers:

At age 65:

$0.7 m @ 5%

$9.0m @ 10%

$80 m @ 15%

$600m @ 20%

'Now, unless I just put you to sleep, I suspect you're thinking that's one hell of a big difference,' continued The Oracle. 'I agree ... these four numbers clearly illustrate the profound difference that getting these three key leverage points right can make. And don't forget, you're not the only beneficiary of this process. Imagine the difference you can begin to make in the life of others with that level of resources at your disposal!

'So, no more excuses,' he said with playful gusto, 'especially from those who claim they don't understand money and finance. That's not a valid excuse. These seven laws are all you need to understand, and they are more than manageable for anyone. You certainly don't need to have a sophisticated understanding of finance.'

Wow – for me this conversation was quite a revelation. I had no real understanding of what a huge difference a few simple factors could make. All the time spent dreaming about what life could be like if I won the lottery, and yet I could deliver a similar outcome myself, with a significantly higher level of probability, by putting a few simple steps into place. And largely automated ones at that. Sure, it would require a little time to bear fruit, but fortunately that was something I still had. It made me feel sick to think of how little I had already achieved to date, though. Imagine if I had started saving 20% of everything I earned from the day I earned my first dollar; I would already be well on the way to being wealthy, I suspect. Which made me think … *I have a bone to pick with my parents when I see them next.* How come they didn't teach me this earlier? Although I suspect I know the answer to that question. If I think about the state of their own finances, their own lack of financial freedom, I guess they themselves don't understand what it is I just discovered. *Oh well,* I thought, *thank goodness I am learning this now and not in another ten years' time.*

Continually increasing your earning capacity

There was a fair amount of chatter among the gathered crowd, sharing similar thoughts to my own I suspected, then a young guy in the middle of the room put up his hand.

'Can I ask, what's the best way to ensure you continually increase your earning capacity? I assume that would not be an easy thing to achieve. Can you tell us more about that?'

That was a great question. This did appear to be the most complex of the seven laws, and I was also very keen to understand it better.

'Well, yes of course!' responded The Oracle. 'I agree it is not an easy thing to achieve, but what things of value are ever easy to do at first? At least you are asking the right question, though. Well done! That being, "how do I do it?" Many just assume it's not possible, and therefore ignore it, but it is.

'If, for example, you start out in life on a salary of $40,000 or generating a business income of $40,000, a 15% growth rate would assume that doubles in approximately five years. Is that possible? Of course it is. Many do it. I'm not saying that degree of growth is necessary, but if you want to achieve it or more, then I recommend three things:

'First, ensure the work you are doing meets our criteria of *Great Work*. Second, do that Great Work within a "star company"; and third, deliver 10 times more value than you cost.

'Putting these three principles into action will give you the best chance of continually increasing your earning capacity, whether that be as an employee or business owner.'

I scrawled these down:

Do Great Work.

Do that Great Work within star company.

Deliver 10 x more value than you cost.

'What constitutes Great Work? Well, hopefully you remember that this sits at the intersection of the seven elements I touched on earlier.' The Oracle listed them again:

1. 'I love doing it.

2. 'It's unique or I can do it uniquely well.

3. 'The world really wants or needs it.

4. 'I can make good money doing it.

5. 'It forces me to continually grow and evolve.

6. 'I can do it with great people in a great place.

7. 'It will not harm the planet or other people on the planet.

'Given this has already been dealt with, I will not dwell on it further now. It is however a crucial aspect, as it gives you the motivation and passion to dedicate the time and effort you will need to be successful, and it also ensures that what you are offering is unique and highly valued.

'As for *doing your Great Work in a star company*, this is a really crucial factor. Not doing this is the main reason most people cannot achieve this higher level of earnings growth. The key principle at play here is, not all companies are created equal. In fact, most people will work very hard in businesses going nowhere, while a few will create a great deal with very little. Why? Well, the few who create so much either buy, build or work in a *star company* – a company that is the clear market leader in a high-growth market niche.'

The Oracle returned to the whiteboard and drew a simple four-box matrix, into which he placed a star, a dog, a cow and a question mark. He then proceeded to write the words *Relative position (market share)* and *Business growth rate* on the x and y axes respectively.

The BCG Matrix

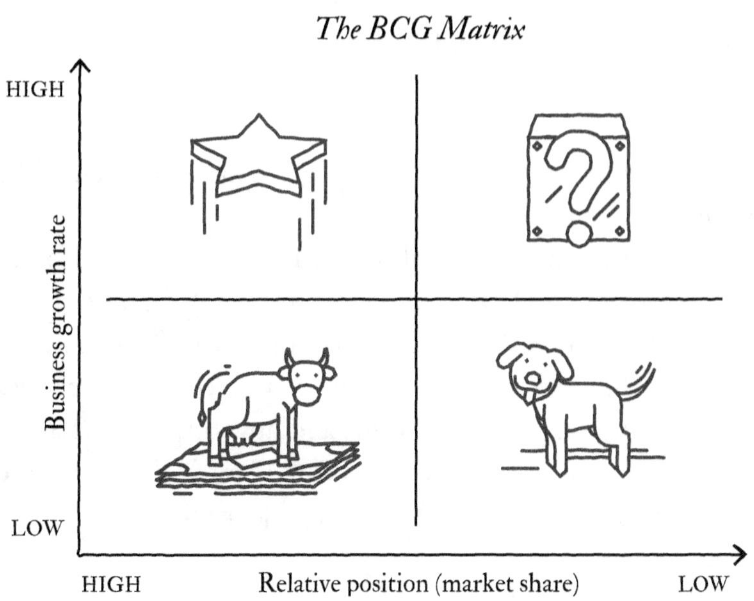

'This is a concept captured beautifully in this diagram originating from the Boston Consulting Group,' he said. 'What makes these star companies unique,' he continued, pointing to the upper-left quadrant, 'is that – because they are the dominant business in a fast-growing market – the overall odds of business success are stacked significantly in their favor. They also typically enjoy far greater profit margins and profit growth, and the ability to reward their employees handsomely as they grow.

'If I am a brilliant employee or the owner of a business that commands a small share of a declining market – what we might call a *dog*,' said The Oracle, pointing to the bottom-right quadrant, 'then it's unlikely I will be able to achieve significant growth in my income or earnings over the next ten years, as the company simply won't have the profits or profit growth to support that. In a star company the outcome is likely to be quite different,' he said with some confidence.

'So, it's all about both working hard and working smart. A little bit of forethought can go a long way in this regard. Ask yourself at the outset: what type of business is likely to offer an ongoing array of new and exciting opportunities? I suspect it's not a *cash cow*. What type of business is likely to be in a position to reward you handsomely for your effort if you do a great job? I suspect it's not a *dog*!

'Your best opportunity to drive your earning capacity is to do your Great Work in a star company, either one you are building yourself or as an employee.'

Wow, that's interesting, I thought. I had never heard of this principle before, and I didn't know anybody who was intentionally applying it. I did recall, however, how often I had contemplated the life of the city's bus drivers who navigated the streets with such skill through peak-hour traffic and how little they earned in comparison to an airline pilot who could largely do their job on cruise control. In this context the principle made a lot of sense to me; we're all going to work hard (well, most of us), but the reward for effort will vary greatly depending on where you apply yourself.

'Finally,' said The Oracle, disrupting my thoughts, 'in relation to our third principle: if you continually *create ten times more value than you cost*, a multiple of this magnitude will produce an ongoing vacuum that will forever suck you onwards and upwards. People who never do any more than they get paid for will never get paid for any more than they do. You don't get paid per hour. You get paid for the value you bring per hour.

'Although this magnitude of value creation will progressively get harder and harder to pull off as your income rises, you must simply view this as a challenge to continually compound your skills.

'That's what I like about this third principle – it forces you to keep getting better and better. In business the Peter Principle is a well-know occurrence. It suggests we all rise to our level of incompetence. What I like about our approach in step eight is the way it overcomes this phenomena. The desire to continually increase your earning capacity forces you to find a way to repeatedly reset your level of competence far beyond what it might otherwise have been.

'I hope that provides good food for thought,' said The Oracle, rubbing his hands together, 'without trivializing its difficulty, as this is clearly one of the hardest aspects to pull off out of what we have discussed here tonight. But you will have the opportunity to make this a focus. If you think back over our seven laws to financial freedom, this is the only one that requires real effort.

'By narrowing down the focus of what's important in life and automating or habitualizing so many of the steps required to achieve success, you free up time and energy to be able to make areas like this your focus. And, when you focus on something with the right mindset at the outset, you are likely to get quite good at it.'

The Oracle proceeded to add this step eight to the Life Plan.

> **Step 1: I have committed to a divine and audacious intention**
> I am here to realize my full potential and help all those I come into contact with realize theirs. I will do this by: Loving and being loved. Doing my Great Work. Maintaining a healthy body and mind and reconnecting to the spirit. Securing my financial freedom. Enjoying the journey.

> **Step 2:**
> I have embraced a new set of limitless beliefs
> *The 12 Core Beliefs*

> **Step 3:**
> I act in alignment with my virtuous Code of Conduct
> *The A to Z of Life*

> **Step 4: I rest knowing what I seek is already mine**

> **Step 5: I have immersed myself in the seven great love affairs**

> **Step 6: I am doing my Great Work**

> **Step 7: I practice the 10 steps of perfect health and transcendence**

> **Step 8: I have secured my financial freedom by implementing the seven laws**

... and then turned back to the group.

'Now for our final step to conclude the process ... '

Step Nine

I STAY ON TRACK, LEVERAGE MYSELF AND ENJOY THE JOURNEY

'Finally, we have reached our ninth and final step. But it's not time to celebrate just yet … ,' cautioned The Oracle. 'I still need to convey some pretty important information here, so keep your wits about you. If you stuff up this last step, you're likely to stuff up *everything*, and this one is easy to stuff up, so stick with me a little longer.

'Step nine is all about staying on track, leveraging yourself and enjoying the journey despite the numerous problems that arise to seemingly thwart our progress. So, let's split the discussion into three parts, starting with the need to enjoy the journey.'

Enjoy the journey

The Oracle walked over to the board and drew a gradually ascending path with numerous ups and downs. He then pointed to the wiggly part of the drawing.

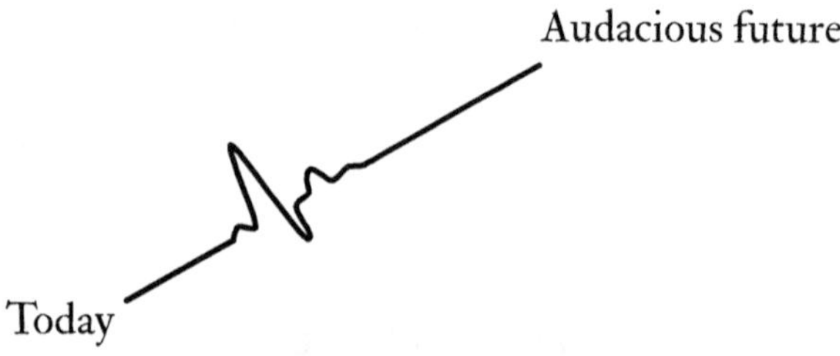

'The world can be a challenging and difficult place to live in and a difficult place to navigate our way through at the best of times. If you have set yourself an audacious intention – as I hope you have, or that you will – then there will be even more challenges than usual on the horizon. That's what these ups and downs convey. But that's only natural and part of the game so you need to be at peace with that.

'Interestingly, once you accept this reality, you can transcend it, and it will cease to cause you any real concern. The fact that you encounter another challenge will no longer matter because it was expected. That's a good place to get to. After all, what's the point of setting yourself an audacious intention if you are not going to enjoy the journey? So, change your mindset.

Happiness is a choice. It really is. I remember the first time I read a statement to this effect I didn't really believe it, but now things are different. I realize now that happiness really is a choice. There's going to be stress in your life, but it's your choice whether you view that as a positive or negative experience. View it as a positive and you can be happy.

'Edith Eger, an Auschwitz survivor who endured unimaginable horrors and hardship and later became a psychologist, said:

Our painful experiences aren't a liability – they're a gift. They give us perspective and meaning, an opportunity to find our unique purpose and our strength. We have a choice: to pay attention to what we've lost or to pay attention to what we still have. Over time I learned that I can choose how to respond to the past. I can be miserable, or I can be hopeful – I can be depressed, or I can be happy. We always have that choice.

Wow, I thought to myself. *I can only begin to imagine what hardships she must have endured, and to emerge with that perspective is truly inspiring.*

The Oracle continued. 'When you face problems, see them as challenges, and rather than turning and running as others might, take up the challenge. Accept all the challenges that come your way, not just the ones you like. The universe will send you a challenge where you need teaching, where you are not yet healed. Lean into those challenges, don't withdraw. Rather than wishing the task was easier, wish that you were better. Don't ask, "Why me?" Ask, "What do I do now?"'

This is a timely reminder, I thought to myself. I often found myself simply wishing that things were easier. Thinking, *why me?*

'As soon as the challenge appears, and its existence is duly acknowledged, place your attention back onto your *intention*, rather than allowing yourself to be consumed by the problem. Don't ignore the problem, but equally don't make it your focus. It's simply a roadblock that you need to work around as you ceaselessly flow forward.

'It might feel like the odds are stacked against you, but take some solace in the knowledge that, throughout history, the underdog has typically won against all odds. David will typically defeat Goliath, assuming he accepts his weaknesses and chooses an unconventional strategy that plays to his unique strengths.

'Confront the darkness within and without and seek to go beyond. You must go forward if you are to take what is rightfully yours,' said The Oracle with a discernible twinkle in his eye. 'Although things might at first appear bad, take comfort in the thought that they could always get worse,' he said jokingly, 'and when they are worse, find hope in the thought that things are so bad they can only get better!

'The world is a chaotic and at times dangerous place, full of improbable and unpredictable events. You can't control the external environment, bad stuff will find you, but ideally by following the *Ninefold Path* you will avoid much of it,' he said with a mixture of warmth and experience.

'When bad things do happen, however, take the lesson and recover quickly. Get back on the horse, so to speak, and relish the opportunity to grow. See it as desirable, even necessary. Know that it is making you stronger.

'You do not need to fall victim to post-traumatic stress. There is such a thing as post-traumatic growth too, you know! You are built to withstand a great deal of stress. Like the Japanese art of Kintsugi, you can emerge stronger and more beautiful in the places that you were broken. Just as human bones get stronger when subjected to stress and tension, so will you.

'I get the idea that it would be preferable to live life without all these ups and downs, but this is the cycle of life at play. By way of example, does anyone recognize this?' He drew a line on the board similar to the previous one, only this time it was horizontal, so it looked just like a beating heart going into cardiac arrest.

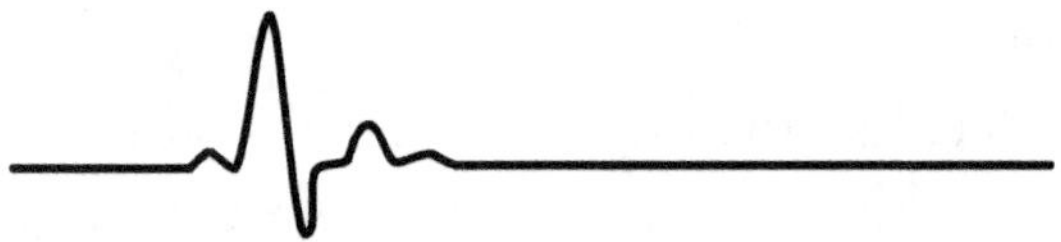

'Well, that's what you get when the ups and downs, the highs and lows, cease,' he said, accentuating the effect by slowly extending the long, flat line. 'You don't want to go there, I can assure you. That would be *deadly* boring.'

His point clearly hit its mark, as laughter broke out around the room. He waited until it subsided, and I reflected. How often I'd wished life were easier, when in reality I should just embrace the journey and enjoy the ride. After all, the rollercoaster is always a lot more fun than the teacup ride.

'"But these are not easy times," you might say. "He is asking a lot of us at a time when things are difficult in the world." To this I would offer an alternative frame of reference that might be more helpful, and ultimately more truthful,' said The Oracle. 'That being: this time, like all times, is a good one if you know what to do with it. And now you do know what to do with it.'

Stay on track

'But through all of this, it's important that you stay on track,' counseled The Oracle. 'You will have set yourself a pretty big agenda here, so you will need to be very skilled in how you go about achieving it. You are more than capable of achieving what needs to done, but you will need to be highly effective in how you tackle each day.

'So, what can we do about that? Well, I would highly recommend the following,' said the Oracle, with a note of excitement.

'**Firstly**, I would recommend you tap into the awesome benefits of visualisation.

'Reconnect with your intention each day through the process of visualization, which we first spoke about in step four.

'Allocate a time each morning to enjoy your intention, contemplating it, reveling in its delightful details. Loving it. Recognize that this is your new reality. Give thanks for it – the elements that you already have and the new.

'**Secondly**, go out into the world and, when faced with a choice, take the path that is more likely to bring you closer to your intention. And, if the universe offers you up an opportunity, make sure you act on it. This is what I call taking *inspired action*.

'"Coincidence is God's way of remaining anonymous," said Einstein. I think there is great wisdom in that statement,' said The Oracle.

'The universe is your friend and will conspire to help you, but it must work *through you* to get things done. *It possesses no other hands but yours*, so is relying on you to take action. You can't sit at the base of the mountain and simply think yourself to the top.

'**Thirdly**, when the day is done, observe it from a distance. Get into the habit of *daily reflection*, which – like visualization – is a highly underutilized process, used by a small handful of high-performing individuals.

'When you go to bed each night, reflect briefly on the day as a neutral observer. It will only take 10 minutes to replay the day like a movie in your mind. As you watch the day unfold, confirm if you acted in line with your **virtuous Code of Conduct** and your **new limitless beliefs**, or did you violate this intent and revert to your old ways of thinking and being?

'As you consider the events of your day, praise yourself where you did well and acknowledge where you could improve. Learn over time not to be critical of yourself for what you might consider to be less-than-perfect behavior, simply note that there is room for improvement and make a commitment to improve.

'Realize that the ability to stand back and objectively reflect on your life is uniquely human and an essential ingredient in living a *remarkable* as opposed to an *ordinary* life. Understand that the very act of observing a behavior tends to change that behavior for the better. Appreciate that when you consciously focus on the manner in which you are conducting your life, you will perform better and better.

'Current weakness isn't a life sentence. Everything you are aspiring to do and become can be learnt, practiced, improved and ultimately mastered. And once you do, everything in your life will change for the better.

'If for instance you identify a breach of your Code of Conduct, such as a lack of *fearlessness*, pause and quietly summon the positive emotional memories you have of that quality. Stay with that experience for a few minutes. Let it become part of you and flow through you. Focus on this until you have a clear sense of its meaning and a clear sense of acting in alignment. As you become more aware of the *fearlessness* inside you, you will align yourself with that force. Slowly but steadily, you will find that the higher qualities you seek will increasingly enter your life.

'Be aware that we all have an inner thermostat setting that determines how much success we will allow ourselves to enjoy, and that setting is likely to be below the audacious intent we have set for ourselves. This limit gets set low early in our lives, at a time when we could not think for ourselves, as part of the round one and two programming process.

'Unfettered, we will sabotage ourselves when we begin to exceed that imagined upper limit. So, you will need to keep breaking through these self-imposed limitations by shining a light on them. In that way you will be able to enjoy a continuous upward spiral.'

Leverage Yourself

'The Greek philosopher Archimedes once said, "Give me a lever long enough and a place to stand, and I can move the world." By using leverage, we humans can multiply our effectiveness and significantly increase the outcome achieved in proportion to the effort applied. Leverage has helped make our life what it is today, and one of the things you need to leverage most is your time. In that regard, I would recommend six things,' said The Oracle.

Firstly, accept those things that you cannot control, your circle of concern, and focus instead on those things you can control – your circle of influence.' The Oracle got to his feet and drew two circles, one within the other. The inner circle he labeled *Circle of Influence*, the outer circle he labeled *Circle of Concern*.

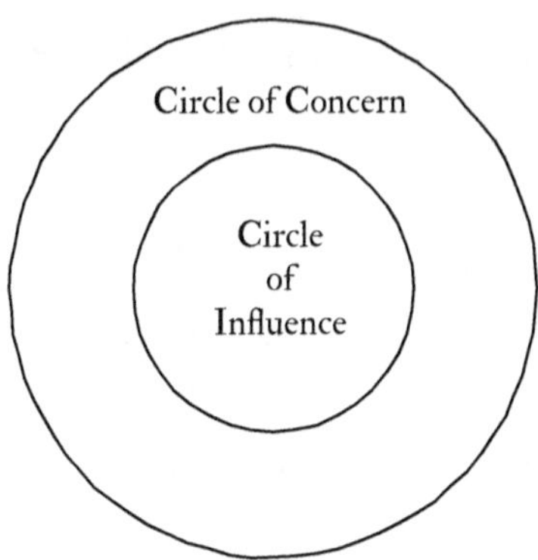

'As you can see, one is much larger than the other. To lead a remarkable life, you will need to focus your emotional and intellectual energies and actions on the smaller inner circle, expanding it where possible so the things you once simply worried about are now things you have found a way to do something about.

'Having done that, the **second** thing I suggest you do,' said the Oracle, 'is recognize that even within your circle of influence, not all tasks are of equal importance. This is where Pareto's Law or the 80/20 principle comes into play: the concept that 80% of results typically come from only 20% of inputs.'

The Oracle now drew a couple of columns side by side on the whiteboard, which he then carved into two unequal sections to illustrate how spending your time on the vital few things, as opposed to the trivial many, will in fact achieve 80% of what you are after.

The Pareto principle of time versus result

'Imagine,' said the Oracle, looking proudly at his latest work of art, 'doing only 20% of the things you currently do and still achieving 80% of the outcome. You could add hours to your day, compounding your health, wealth and happiness,' he said, sporting a wide grin.

'**Thirdly**,' continued the Oracle with a fitting sense of urgency, 'now you are clear on what needs to be done, delegate and out-source as many lower-value activities as possible to give yourself more time to do the few things that provide the highest payoff. Recognize that you cannot achieve what you need to achieve without the help of others. Self-sufficiency is another word for poverty.

'**Fourthly**, having palmed off to others all you can, I encourage you to schedule time to do those things you cannot delegate. Think of it this way,' said the Oracle, drawing another large square on the whiteboard, which he then divided into four quadrants. 'In the top left you have the urgent but unimportant. In the top right the urgent and important. The bottom left the non-urgent and unimportant. And finally, in the bottom right the non-urgent but important.'

Zone 1 Urgent Unimportant	*Zone* 3 Urgent Important
Zone 2 Non-urgent Unimportant	*Zone* 4 Non-urgent Important

'These four zones are available to the average person. The difference is, those that live a remarkable life spend their days in Zones 3 and 4. And the more time you spend in Zone 4,' he added, 'the less time you will need to spend in Zone 3, which will be a welcome relief as you then become master of your day rather than running from fire to fire. Move beyond the misconception that all urgent things are important and need your immediate attention,' said

The Oracle, taking his seat once more. 'They simply "pretend" to be so. Good time management is not about doing things more efficiently; it is about not doing certain things at all. I find that if I spend the first few hours of each day in Zone 4, my days become far less hectic. If I do the important things first, then all the small, less meaningful tasks can fill in the time that's left.'

'**Fifth**, each time you finish a task then simply ask yourself, *what is the most important thing I can do next?* Then do that.'

'My **final** suggestion is that you will benefit greatly from having a guide,' said The Oracle. 'A guide, not a hero, mind you. You are the hero in this story, so you don't need another one of those, but you do need a guide.

'You see, knowing *what* to do is one thing but knowing *how* to do it is another thing altogether. There are some skills you can learn on your own, but if you are seriously committed to living a remarkable life then the best thing you can do is arrange for first-rate instruction.

'There is *very little sustained performance at the level of excellence* – of any kind, anywhere – *without continuous coaching.* Most people have no idea of what they are truly capable of. That is why the successful among us typically have mentors or coaches – to watch over us and point out the subtle changes that will make all the difference.

'In this fast-moving world of ours, the self-taught person is on an uncertain path indeed. I therefore feel comfortable suggesting that the single most important difference between those who live a *remarkable* life and those who live an *ordinary* life is that those who live a remarkable life seek out a guide.

'After all, Frodo had Gandalf, Luke Skywalker had Obi-Wan Kenobi, Harry Potter had Dumbledore. All guides who had been there and done that. Someone who had already taken the hero's journey and emerged victorious. Someone they could respect and trust, and learn from.

'You can't solve everything on your own. At least not for now.

In summary

The Oracle allowed a moment for his message to sink in, and then stole a quick glance at the clock on the wall – which was somewhat ironic given the topic of discussion.

He then got to his feet and drew a new diagram on the board. At its centre he noted the key belief of enjoying the journey regardless, and around the perimeter he placed the nine actions for staying on track and leveraging yourself. Looking at it like this tied it all together nicely.

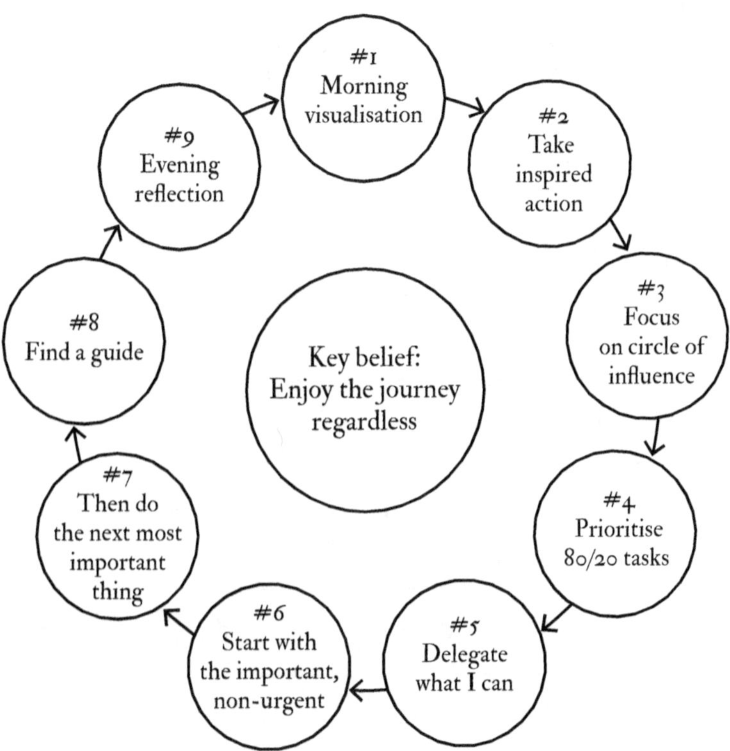

'Time is the most precious resource we have, but it is the gift that we tend to abuse the most. You need to change that. Make sure you use it wisely and apply what you have learnt here tonight,' he said, pointing at the newly created diagram.

He then turned to the whiteboard and proceeded to add this final step to the Life Plan.

Step 1: I have committed to a divine and audacious intention
I am here to realize my full potential and help all those I come into contact with realize theirs. I will do this by: Loving and being loved. Doing my Great Work. Maintaining a healthy body and mind and reconnecting to the spirit. Securing my financial freedom. Enjoying the journey.

Step 2:
I have embraced a new set of limitless beliefs
The 12 Core Beliefs

Step 3:
I act in alignment with my virtuous Code of Conduct
The A to Z of Life

Step 4: I rest knowing what I seek is already mine

Step 5: I have immersed myself in the seven great love affairs

Step 6: I am doing my Great Work

Step 7: I practice the 10 steps of perfect health and transcendence

Step 8: I have secured my financial freedom by implementing the seven laws

Step 9: I stay on track, leverage myself and enjoy the journey

I looked at the *Life Plan* that had quietly emerged over the course of the evening – imagining myself at the center – and grew rather excited at the prospect of making this a reality. Of having this become my life. It felt like a very clear, concise and compelling plan.

New daily routine

The Oracle continued: 'To help you make this plan a reality, use your new daily routine to make time for the things that matter. Turn your early morning into a *Miracle Morning* by allocating time for meditation, time for exercise and time for visualization. In your *Dynamic Day*: allow time to do your important but non-urgent work at the beginning of the day, and then do the next most important thing you need to do, and then then the next, and then the next, throughout the remainder of the day. As part of your *Engaging Evening*: allow time to spend with your family and friends, and just before you drift into your *Satisfying Sleep*, undertake a quick process of reflection. Support this all with a couple of days focused on rest and rejuvenation, spending quality time with family and friends, the pursuit of hobbies, time in nature, gaining new knowledge. What I like to refer to as a Wonderful Weekend.' The Oracle added these items to the simple weekly outline he had drawn earlier ...

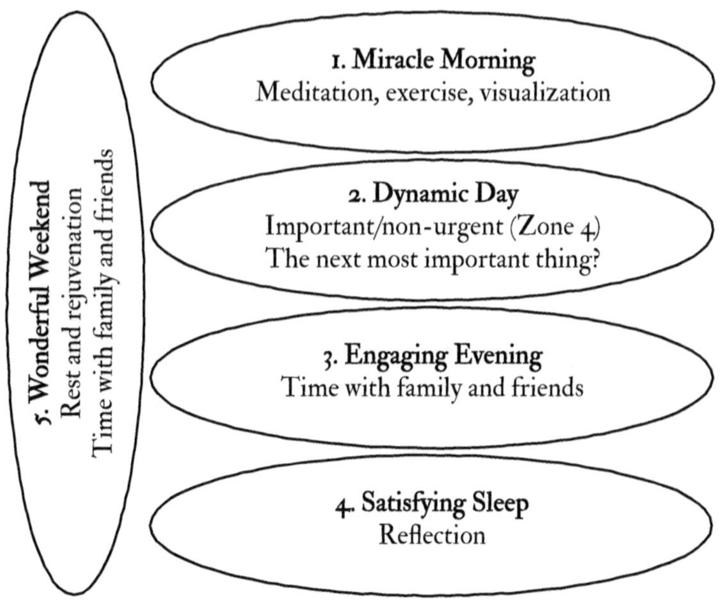

... and then turned back to the group. 'As you well know, that was our ninth and final step,' he announced with a hint of sadness.

I too felt a slight sadness that our time was coming to an end, but was also excited at the prospect of putting it all into action and somewhat pleased that there were no additional steps I had to master.

'I am hoping this all makes sense to you. But what other questions do you have?' enquired The Oracle.

Part Three

QUESTIONS AND ANSWERS

A flurry of hands were raised in response ...

Pleasure

'You're encouraging us to contemplate a pretty extraordinary life for ourselves,' stated an older man near the back of the room, 'but are we at risk of seeking too much pleasure in this day and age?'

'Right!' The Oracle responded. 'A stoic among our ranks,' he said playfully, provoking laughter from the crowd, and then he continued.

'I agree that our primary goal in life is not pleasure, as some would have you think. It's the pursuit of what we find meaningful. But that does not mean you don't participate in pleasurable activities along the way – the ecstasy of another's body against our own, the joy of sharing a drink with friends, the bliss of a well-deserved meal.

'These are all essential and admirable parts of living life to the full. Although you are a spiritual being, you are having a physical experience and should make every effort to enjoy the benefits of that while it lasts. By all means participate in the physicality of life.

'You just need to keep in mind ... which is probably the point you are making and one I agree with ... ,' said The Oracle, turning to the person who had asked the question, 'that you will often need to show some restraint. To not just do what is pleasurable, but rather do what is required and sometimes less pleasurable in the moment, to achieve your pleasurable intention.

'If, for instance, I want to achieve great health then I will need to exercise and eat predominately healthy food. Both less pleasurable activities than the alternatives at times, but they lead to a pleasurable outcome – that being great health.'

There were a number of heads nodding in the audience, signaling understanding and agreement with what had been said.

The opinions of others

'I really love the steps that you have set out for us, thank you for that,' said a young woman near the front of the room, 'but what do you suggest we do about the opinions of others in all of this. I know when I leave here tonight and attempt to apply the things I have learned, some of my friends and family will mock me and challenge me rather than supporting the changes I am planning to make in my life.'

Several people in the crowd were nodding in agreement. I also found myself a little concerned about how any changes I was considering might be received.

'That's a great question,' said The Oracle. 'In response let me say please, please, please – I implore you – only measure your life using an *inner* scorecard. Do not seek public approval or recognition from others. How other people view you is nowhere near as important as how you view yourself.

'You now have a fairly comprehensive reference point. Your Purpose, your Vision of Perfection, and your Vivid Descriptor all clearly articulate what success looks like for you. Your Code of Conduct clarifies the behavior you expect of yourself. Your new limitless beliefs clarify the way you wish to view the world. Each time you are in any doubt simply refer back to these.

'First and foremost, you need to be true to yourself. There has never been anyone quite like you, and I can assure you there never will be again. You are certainly one of a kind, and here for a reason. So, don't try to fit in – you were born to stand out. Speak your own truth, define your own version of success. Your difference is your destiny.

'How am I going?' asked The Oracle, with a smile to the audience. 'A few corny little catch phrases I know, but they are memorable. Have I convinced you yet?' But before we could answer he continued …

'By all means listen to others. I think it is very important to constantly take on board the feedback and opinions of others you trust. But ultimately you need to follow your own unique path guided by your spirit. If the path you choose is not what others suggest or approve of, then don't worry about what others think or say and certainly don't worry about looking good. As long as you are doing what's required to achieve *your* audacious intention, and you are living in accordance with your beliefs and Code of Conduct, you can take comfort and be content that you are on the right track.

'If, because of living in this new manner, you make enemies, it probably means you've stood up for something. If others don't see your worth, it doesn't mean you are worthless. You do not need to prove yourself in life, but you do need to fully express yourself.

'Take the path less traveled, or even better, create a whole new path, a third option if that's what it will take to be whole rather than perfect. This will make all the difference.'

The greater good

'What about the greater good, the broader community?' asked another man. 'To what extent should we sacrifice our self-interest for others?'

'Brilliant,' replied the Oracle. 'I really appreciate that question because there is still much work to be done in that regard, so thank you for the opportunity to answer this.

'Society needs to change. We really do! The fabric of our communities, the very fabric of our society is being undermined by extreme individualism.

'I'm going to go out on a bit of a limb here and suggest that most of you are also guilty. Guilty of not yet loving all living beings without partiality or bias. Yet that's where you need to get to.

'And, please don't just sit there in furious agreement thinking that this is indeed something *others* need to address, without also acknowledging that this is something you seriously need to change about yourself also.

'If my experience is any judge, you aren't getting this right – and I admit I still don't always get it right either – so please sit up and take notice.'

There was a shuffling of bodies in chairs as people responded to the affront.

'Most of you will have a circle of concern: your family, friends and maybe a smattering of those in need who have caught your attention, but that's it.

'Most of you still see yourselves, your family and your circle of friends as the center of the universe. In this regard, you assume, quite wrongly, that other people, events and things derive their significance primarily from the way in which they affect you.

'You assume your friends are important because they are an important part of your life, while strangers are not so important because they do not directly affect your life.

'Well, that needs to change. You need to make it your goal to become a source of benefit to everyone and everything. We are all part of one big family. As Martin Luther King once warned us, we will either learn to "live together as brothers, or perish together as fools".

'While the priority for any society is freedom, we need to be willing to give up some personal freedom for the greater good. We appear to be separate, but we are all rooted in the same source. We should therefore strive together for the common good, re-establish a sense of the oneness of humanity – live in harmony with one another ...

'The best societies are those that do not simply offer personal freedom but lessen the lottery of life by giving fair chances and justice to all. They give up some personal liberty for the needs of the whole.'

Intelligence

'I find all of this very motivating,' blurted out a young guy at the back of the room, causing everyone to turn in his direction. 'I really do want to leave here and go out into the world and do great things, but I often feel I'm not smart enough to compete with others and succeed in this world.'

'Well, you are certainly not alone in that regard', responded The Oracle. 'I often feel that way as well, and then I simply remind myself that I'm as smart as I need to be.

'Intelligence has little to do with success. You don't need to be a rocket scientist to do well in this world. Fortunately ... or mercifully in my case,' joked The Oracle, 'life is *not* a game where the person with the highest IQ always wins.

'In fact, in most cases it's harder for a highly tuned Ferrari to navigate the world than a simple, well-used and slightly dented all-terrain 4WD.'

That sounds hopeful, I thought, reflecting on my own modest level of intelligence.

'That's not to say there isn't an important role for intelligence to play in enriching the lives of others – there is,' added The Oracle. 'But it's not the only role of importance.

'The big take away for you,' said The Oracle, turning back to the person who had originally asked the question, 'and for any of you that feel the same way,' he now said addressing the room as a whole, 'is to rest easy in the knowledge that, regardless of what your thing is, you will be every bit as capable as you need to be to do it to a very high level of excellence. Your best will be good enough.

'What you truly desire and what your true self aspires to achieve is something you are more than capable of achieving. If not, the desire would not have been present in the first place.

'Keep in mind that success in life is a system, not an event. Follow the system outlined tonight and your level of intelligence will be more than enough to deliver the success you desire.'

Mistakes in the past

'But what if we have really mucked things up previously?' said another young male.

'Once again, you'll be fine,' shot back The Oracle. 'We all have at some point.

'Your past doesn't have any power over the present. You are not your past; you are a product of the decisions you make from this point forward. Although you can't change the start, you can certainly make a brand-new ending.

'You will, however, need to accept that the past is over and forgive yourself and others for any wrong done. You can't change what has happened, you can't change what you did or what was done to you. But you *can* choose how you live now. See those things that you might have once been ashamed or guilty of as nothing more than a valuable learning experience toward your inevitable and complete success.

'You don't have time to ask, "Why me?" The only relevant question is, "What do I do now?" We all fail our way to success. If we're not failing at some level, it's unlikely that we're even trying. So, think of it as divine redirection rather than failure, and expect that there will be many bumps if you take the hero's journey.

'But don't let that concern you, as the redirections will simply make you stronger. Pain is there to alert you and help direct you. The trick is to find the positive in the negative. Every challenge and every failure can be viewed positively or negatively. You get to choose. What you're thankful for, despite the harm or pain it may have caused, provides fuel in your life going forward. What you continue to admonish will poison both your present and the future. You don't die from the snake bite – you die from its poison circulating through your veins.

'Good times and bad times are only ever a matter of perspective, as this old Chinese fable conveys.'

The Oracle made himself comfortable and then began ...

'The farmer's horse runs away. A neighbor says, "That's bad news."

'The farmer replies, "Good news, bad news, who can say?"

'The horse returns home, bringing another horse with him. Good news, you might say.

'The farmer gives the new horse to his son. He rides it, then he is thrown and breaks his leg badly.

'"So sorry for your bad news," says the concerned neighbor.

'"Good news, bad news, who can say?" replies the farmer.

'A few days later, the Emperor's officials arrive to take every able-bodied young man to fight in the latest imperial war. The farmer's son is written off as a useless cripple and is spared.

'Good news, of course ...

'I like that story,' says The Oracle, pausing to let the ancient wisdom sink in.

Major setbacks

'You talk about bouncing back from setbacks, but what happens when you are faced with major loss in your life?'

'That is a very good question,' said The Oracle, 'and I appreciate you raising it, for I have probably not been clear enough in that regard. You make a good point. Every so often you will face a major loss in life that gives rise to a valid, necessary and prolonged period of grief.

'While there is not necessarily a *correct* way to grieve in these circumstances, five stages are common: denial, anger, bargaining, depression and, finally, acceptance.

'Keep in mind that when facing major loss in your life, it's both natural and normal to feel these emotions. They will help you to accept what has happened, and in the process make you stronger.

'Jamie Anderson put this beautifully when he said:

Grief, I've learned, is really just love. It's all the love you want to give but cannot. All that unspent love gathers up in the corner of your eyes, the lump in your throat, and in the hollow part of your chest. Grief is just love with no place to go.

'The idea that grief is love with no place to go is a powerful concept. When confronted with a major loss, feel the grief, recognize it as love, and then when the time is right let it pass through you,' said The Oracle.

The room remained silent for an extended period, taking in what had been said.

Friendship

'I feel like friendships play an important role in helping us deal with life's challenges,' said a woman to my right. 'You spoke about loving your friends earlier as one of the seven key love affairs. Can you tell us more about this?'

The Oracle smiled. 'We all need a small group of well-selected and highly valued friends. So, make friends with people who want the best for you in life, and keep those friendships a constant part of your journey.

'As for the toxic relationships, discard them! You certainly don't need them weighing you down. People change, circumstances change and the dynamics of a friendship can also change. Not every friend will be a friend for life.

'Some friends are with you for a season, some for a reason, and some for life. Don't wrestle with those that come and go for a season, appreciate those who come for a reason, and revel in the joy of those who are with you for life.'

Life partner

'While we are on the topic of friends,' asked a woman to my left, 'what about partners? More and more people seem to be staying single longer ... do we need a partner?

That's an interesting question, I thought, contemplating my own status and lack of desire to commit to anything too long term.

'Well ... I hope you're not setting me up here,' said The Oracle lightheartedly in response. 'I'm assuming that's not your partner sitting next to you.'

The woman laughed in response, and then assured The Oracle that he was safe to speak his mind.

'Very well then,' he said, 'my belief is you certainly don't *need* a partner.' He placed a lot of emphasis on the word need. 'You don't need anything outside of yourself to make you whole. But, by finding the right partner you can certainly double the joy and halve the sorrow of life.

'Get it wrong, however, and you are in for a world of pain. That's why for many, this is the most important choice we will ever make.

'In physics, when two waves move toward one another in phase, they will merge and magnify, the resultant wave being twice the size of the original. This phenomenon is referred to as *constructive interference*. On the other hand, when the same two waves come together inharmoniously, they cancel each other out. Instead of the wave energy doubling, it dissipates. This phenomenon is called *destructive interference*.

'Good relationships are all about *constructive* interference – the merging of the right two people can double your power, rather than reduce it. Relationships are not here to save or fix us. You don't need a partner to be complete or balanced in life, but you can certainly enlarge yourself and your life with the right one.

'A good relationship can be a safe and enriching place for mutual evolution. An even better place to be seen, heard and fully express your true self.'

Parenting

'What of parenting?' called out another audience member. 'Do you have anything to say about that?'

'Well, in terms of all the key relationships in your life,' responded The Oracle, 'this is indeed the hardest one of all. Not because it's hard to love our children, that's easy, but because it's hard to love them and raise them at the same time.

'We all want to raise healthy, happy, well-adjusted children, but none of us are given an instruction manual at birth, so it's important to pause and think about what might be required to increase the probability of success.

'Anyone can learn from their own experience, but it is far better to learn from the experience of others. The wise will always endeavor to understand how things work ahead of time. They look for a better system than trial and error. I would encourage you to do the same. Search out some proven strategies to increase the probability of success.

'While we don't have time to go into these now, I do have a list for those who are interested.* It's a framework you can apply to increase your probability of success as a parent.'

He held it up for all to see. 'Feel free to pick up a copy as you leave the room. I hope these strategies help to make the task far more understandable for you.'

---

*   Refer to the appendix.

The environment

'... And the environment,' asked another. 'What are your thoughts on that?'

The Oracle adjusted his posture as if he were reconnecting with an invisible force.

'Without it there could be no life. "I am I plus my surroundings, and if I don't preserve the latter, I do not preserve myself," said the Spanish philosopher José Ortega y Gasset.

'A perspective captured so persuasively by Chief Seattle, in a letter he purportedly wrote to the US President in 1855, in response to a request to purchase their land. In this he said the following, among other things ...

... every part of the earth is sacred ... every shining pine needle, every sandy shore, every mist in the dark woods, every meadow, every humming insect ...

The sap which courses through the trees is of the same essence as the blood that courses through our veins. The shining water that moves in the streams and rivers is not just water, it is the blood of our ancestors. We are part of the earth and it is part of us. The perfumed flowers, and all other flora, are our sisters. The bear, the deer, the great eagle, and all other fauna, are our brothers. We all belong to the same family.

The earth is our mother; what befalls the earth, befalls all the sons of the earth. The earth does not belong to man, man belongs to the earth. All things are connected like the blood that unites us all. Man did not weave the web of life; he is merely a strand in it. Whatever he does to the web, he does to himself.

The Oracle stopped. He took in the hushed silence.

Clearly these words were close to his heart, and he was noticeably moved by them. You could sense his profound love of the planet, and his connection to nature.

'So, love both the planet and all other living beings, people! Love them deeply. As a minimum, ensure you do them no harm, but where you can, go beyond that and help them to flourish once more.'

Leadership and power

'You talk about striving together for the common good, which makes perfect sense,' suggested a young woman, 'but lately we seem to have been let down greatly by the leaders of our institutions, whether in big business, religion or politics. Would you agree that the world seems to be lacking credible leaders at a time when we need them most?'

'In response to that question,' responded The Oracle, 'let me say two things.

'First, although what you say is true, it's important to understand that tomorrow can be better than today, and we all have a personal moral obligation to make it so.

'Second, I would add that you need to be the change you seek. Lead yourself to a better place and you will then be well positioned to influence others, who will, in turn, influence others, and on it goes. Before you know it, *you* will have created significant change yourself, rather than relying on others

'If, for instance, I profoundly influenced 10 people here tonight, who in turn went out into the world and influenced another 10 people, who in turn influenced another 10 people, and on it went 10 times over – do you realize how many people I will have influenced? Well, 10 to the power of 10 people, which equals 10 *billion*. A number that comfortably captures the entire population of the world. How cool is that? I could do something here tonight that ends up impacting the entire planet.

'Small steps can lead to big changes across the globe. *You* can be the leader you seek. You don't need anyone's permission to lead. Just go out there and do it.

'Those who clear the path get to determine the direction of travel. So, don't run from power but, rather, gather it ever so wisely and carefully as the opportunity permits. Power in the hands of a good person can refresh everyone with whom it comes into contact.

Fear

'You talk about fear as though it is something we should rid ourselves of,' said a young guy with long hair near the back of the room. 'But isn't fear a very powerful emotion that can be harnessed to optimize productivity: the fear of failing a university subject, the fear of losing a job, the fear of ill health and the fear of death can motivate us to achieve a better outcome for ourselves in the short and long term?'

'That is a really great question,' said The Oracle, 'and a tough one.

'Here you have two options. Either using fear as a motivator or its opposite, abundance.

'It's a bit like the lure of the dark force versus the light in *Star Wars*. Both are immensely powerful, and one is arguably quicker and easier to access – the dark force – but ultimately one is more powerful and less damaging than the other – the light.

'Same here. Fear works but it is a lousy source of inspiration. If your reasons for engaging in anything are based in fear, or shame, or guilt, although progress in their name may feel like progress it will leave you unsatisfied. When fear or scarcity or guilt is our primary motivator, our efforts will never be truly satisfying. As a consequence, the happiness that we seek along the way will remain elusive.

'Instead, can I suggest you motivate yourself to complete that university assignment, or do well in your work, or eat food that is good for you, with an abundance mindset. Let a desire to do your best be your motivator. A desire to deliver Great Work. A desire to serve others. A desire to display persistence, and live true to your other valued virtues or Code of Conduct.

'Although these motivators may take slightly longer to nurture and develop within yourself, longer term they will leave you significantly more powerful and content.'

Anxiety

'Do you have any thoughts in relation to anxiety?' asked a woman in the audience. 'It now seems to be reaching epidemic proportions within our society. Any thoughts on what we can do to better deal with this?'

'Well, yes I do,' responded The Oracle. 'But what I have to say may surprise you.'

He had my attention. Anxiety was certainly something I needed to eradicate. Far too much of my life was spend in fight, flight or fear, robbing me of the joy that could otherwise be mine.

'I would begin by saying that it's common for people to feel anxious,' said The Oracle. 'So do not be frustrated by the emotion. Accept it. Welcome it.

'But I would then warn you not to indulge it. Particularly because it's not real!'

Not real? *Well, I didn't expect that*, I thought to myself. The Oracle paused, registering a few other rather dubious looking responses among the crowd.

'I accept it *feels* very real,' acknowledged The Oracle, 'but so does a dream at the time. And, just like a dream, it's not. It's not real because the divine cannot be stressed, fearful or anxious. This is simply a construct of the delusional self. There is no stress, fear or anxiety in the world, only people thinking stressfully, fearfully, anxiously.

'The cause of your anxiety is not life itself, although at first it will always appear to be ... it is the commotion that your mind makes about life. As you pull back into the spirit, and away from the mind, the world ceases to be a problem; it's just something you are watching.

'So, when you feel anxious, remind yourself that it is not real, and reconnect to the source, the spirit, once again, and feel that anxiety fall away.'

Addiction

'What do you have to say about drugs?' asked another. 'This appears to be an issue of major concern these days. What are your thoughts on this?'

'I share your concern,' responded The Oracle. 'Drugs, or any form of addiction, are a serious issue. What do we mean when we speak of addiction? Well, it is any regular act that we know is not good for us longer term, but we can't stop ourselves from doing it.

'The addiction may be to drugs, alcohol, sex, pornography, gambling, or shopping. There are a multitude of possible culprits. Some are more harmful than others, but no addiction is healthy, so we should seek to overcome it. At the very least it limits our potential, at worst it will destroy our life altogether.

'I appreciate we all want bliss in our life. But you will never find the answer in addiction. Mastin Kipp has this beautiful expression: "addicts are just looking for God in all the wrong places". I think that makes a lot of sense.

'Taking drugs, or the excessive use of alcohol, as a means to fill a void or mask that pain within you is about as effective as grabbing a scalpel and cutting off your stomach as a way to lose weight. They both work in the short term but have disastrous longer term consequences.

'In the case of drugs, by way of example, your body, your physiology and your nervous system are all irrevocably damaged. Worst of all, your body will continually adapt to the use, so you will forever need more and more just to achieve the same temporary high. That puts you on a vicious cycle of self-destruction, where the original intent becomes an increasingly distant reality.

'A far more effective, profound and lasting outcome can be achieved naturally. The same peace and freedom that you seek from your addiction can be achieved by healing yourself of unprocessed trauma, filling that void within with your own self-love and reconnecting with your true self. Do not attempt to simply mask the pain, you need to resolve it. That's a much more effective way to once again be whole. Remember the madness is in the world, not in you.

'If the issue is more about trying to fit in, then keep in mind that life is not about fitting in – you were born to stand out. Your success will flow when you bring more of yourself to each day and every moment. It will not be because you do what others are doing. Be true to yourself, listen to your own heart and follow your own dreams. Define your own version of success and think beyond the confines of culture.'

Religion

'You talk about success as a system or process, but what about the role of faith and religion?' said a woman near the front. 'What role should they play in our life?'

'Well, that's a complex topic indeed – a vexed question for many, not so vexed for some,' responded The Oracle. 'If we think of religion as not only a collection of beliefs but a way of seeing the world, then we seem to have two paths diverging.

'On one path are the atheists or agnostics, or those I like to refer to as the *individualists*. They do not believe in a God. For them, the universe is all there is, there is no heaven, life is random, and they journey through it as a sole entity, determining their own fate, believing that when you die – that's it. Their motivation stems from their belief that you're on your own, so you had better get out there and make something of yourself.

'On the other path are the *religious*, who believe there is a God who creates and upholds the world and who created humans in his image. Humans are God's chosen creatures and are expected to conquer the elements. If we are good and work hard, we will go to heaven, and, if not, then hell awaits us. We should do our best, but at the end of the day we are all sinners. God is almighty, and people, although loved, are small in comparison to the glory of God.

'The problem with the former is the misguided belief that you are on your own, that you are separate and need to do all the heavy lifting. The problem with the latter is you give up far too much control, it diminishes your significance and delays your magnificence until you are dead.

'There is however a third option that I see emerging strongly. What I call the path of the *spiritualist*.'

Spiritualist? I jotted it down. I'd never heard the term before. Clearly a number of others in the room had not heard it either, if the chatter that subsequently broke out among my neighbors was any indication ...

Spiritualism

'So how might a spiritualist approach life?' came the next question.

That was a question I welcomed as the exact same thought had entered my mind.

'Well, for a start, spiritualists don't think of life as a series of random events,' said The Oracle, 'or something that is being overseen by a central God-like figure. They think of life as a partnership.

'It's not a dog-eat-dog world, focused on survival of the fittest. No, cooperation, collaboration and co-creation are the name of the game. A one–two–three knockout. You clarify the intention, the spirit sets up the opportunity, and you then conclude the process by taking the necessary action.

'You and the spirit can make a powerful team,' said The Oracle. 'Best of all, it's a path that doesn't need a hierarchy, or particular place of worship, or any ordained leaders. It opens up the possibility for an inspiring vision of the world and your role within it.'

A new world view

'So, what might that inspiring vision of the world be?' came the next question, to my great delight as I was really interested in understanding more also.

'Well, it is to see life as a wonderful adventure, full of hope and possibility,' said The Oracle in response. 'With no need for fear and doubt. For the real you cannot be afraid, it cannot be frightened.

'You work harmoniously in collaboration with the *spirit*, that unseen source or intelligent form, that permeates and fills the interspaces of the universe. That unmanifested energy out of which all things emerge.

'You recognize that this is an intelligence far greater than us, there to bring forth what is inside you. Something it desperately wants and needs to do, for ultimately it must work *through you* to get things done.

'You understand that life works better, has more meaning and is eminently more joyous and easier when you reconnect, co-create and live in collaboration with this unseen spirit.

'You realize there is no need to worship another. You are simply seeking to be in vibratory accord with your divine self, your true self – the spirit – and the closer you move to be in alignment with your true self the greater your genius. You are your own healer, hero and leader. If you have to worship anything, you worship nature.

'You know that the whole of life is one, the seen and the unseen, matter and spirit. That the universe is an unbroken, unified whole despite the illusion of being a multitude of separate objects.

'You understand that the world changes when we perceive it differently. Those things that take on the appearance and feel of form are just vibrating energy. The true nature of the world is not solidity, stability, and permanence but perpetual motion.

'As a consequence, you do not grasp or cling to that which is transitionary. You recognize that the most important things in life are invisible. The material is never coveted or overly relied upon. But you do see the physical abundance that surrounds you as something to be appreciated and enjoyed.

'You know life will continually go up and down. It is both predictable and unpredictable. We get both what we want and don't want. You relax into that change and see the world afresh. You can flourish on both the good days and the bad days.

'You appreciate the world as it is, not as you would like it to be. You realize we have limited control over how the cards of life are dealt, but we do control the hand we play once they are.

'As for the people and situations we find most difficult, well you recognize that they are the best teachers in life.

'You see love as the divine power. So, you approach all you do with a simple but powerful question; *how would love respond?* If I loved myself how would I respond? If I loved you how would I respond? If I loved what I was doing how would I respond? And you respond accordingly, knowing that it's never loving that hurts, its not loving.

'You seek to get to the essence or true nature of things and people. You look for the truth behind appearance. Lift the veil of misperception.

'You understand that in quietness all things are answered. So, you use this technique to escape the habits of normal perception and see things as if for the first time. Think beyond the confines of culture.

'You appreciate the only time you ever have is this moment. You appreciate that you are born anew in every moment. You have already had a thousand deaths and a thousand births in this lifetime alone. You leave your past and become your present now, a new person now. And now. And now. And now. And now.'

Who are you?

Wow. I found that very inspiring. So inspiring, I felt compelled to raise my own hand and dig further. Something I would normally not do. 'So tell us again, could you please, who we really are,' I asked rather timidly.

'I would love to,' said The Oracle turning toward me. 'You are a manifestation of the spirit in material form. A divine being having a human experience. Your essential nature is pure immortal energy. You are in this world but not of it.

'Everything is of its source. You are no different. You are not separate from your source. It doesn't require work to become who you are. You simply need to get out of the way, to allow yourself to unfold and to bloom as a flower might by following the steps we are outlining here tonight. No more, no less.'

I really liked this idea. If I shut my eyes and thought of myself in this way, I could see how everything changes. It was going to be important for me to hold onto this, I thought.

What are we truly capable of?

'Let me also add this,' said The Oracle, ignoring the other questions in the room momentarily. 'Can I also remind you once more what you are truly capable of.

'You see, it's not about doing things a little better, it's about reclaiming your true identity, your true nature far beyond what's been claimed thus far.

'You are *not* some small, insignificant and powerless speck within the universe. Quite the contrary – you are the universe, and the universe is within you. That makes you all powerful and limitless; as we all are.

'You are therefore no better than anyone or anything else and no one else is better than you. But, you are capable of manifesting anything you choose with your intention and attention. You are a vehicle for divine expression and you can realize that potential by taking action in the physical world.

'Paradoxically, it is through losing the small self, the false self, and aligning to your true self that your greatest personal power is gained. Far from losing control, this brings to life all your dormant potentialities.'

How should I live my life?

'So if you had to recap for us, in terms of how we should live our lives, what would you say?' asked a softly spoken woman in the front row.

'Well madam,' said The Oracle warmly, "I would say although the world doesn't belong to humans, it does need humans to belong to it. You must therefore engage and make your contribution. Bring forth your precious present, bring forth what is within you, and the best way to do that is by following the *Ninefold Path*. You therefore ...

1. Commit to a divine and audacious intention.

2. Embrace a new set of limitless beliefs.

3. Act in alignment with your virtuous Code of Conduct.

4. Rest knowing what you seek is already yours.

5. Immerse yourself in the seven great love affairs.

6. Do your Great Work.

7. Practice the 10 steps of perfect health and transcendence.

8. Secure your financial freedom by implementing the seven laws.

9. Stay on track, leverage yourself and enjoy the journey.

'No more, no less. It's an agenda that is both simple and challenging, to guide and inspire you. Clear enough for you to fully appreciate why you are here and what it is you must do, yet challenging enough to be forever pursued but never finished. A window into something far bigger than just yourself.

'Such a life would align you with universal values that have been part of the best societies throughout the ages and noticeably absent from the less successful ones. A set of unchanging and universal laws that transcend any particular culture or individual.'

Death

The next question, although unexpected, was a logical progression. 'So, what happens when we die?' I could not see who had asked it, but I was not alone in having my interest sparked.

'Well, we cannot know for sure,' said The Oracle, 'but, like the wave in the ocean, you are likely to simply return to the ocean of energy from whence you came. From which another wave will be formed and then another and another.

'Death is therefore nothing more than the movement of the spirit from one domain to another. But ironically, it is also your greatest friend.

'If you let death in, you will experience firsthand how life comes with it. Its presence brings a welcome and necessary urgency to life. If you live each day as though it could be your last but continue to plan as though you will live forever, you will have mastered one of the great paradoxes of life.'

I thought about that chart of the number of months in a life, which had started me on this journey.

'So, don't let death worry you; it is only a small piece of the whole, a blip in the grand scheme of things. Its great gift is to motivate you to live a life with no regrets, forcing you to seize the day and ensure you do not miss the opportunity to be fabulous.

'As the visionary Steve Jobs once said, death is therefore probably the best invention of life. Remembering that you will be dead soon is the best way to avoid the trap of thinking that you have something to lose in getting out there and living life to the fullest.'

The Oracle took a deep breath. As did I, and everyone else present. There was so much to take in here, but it felt strangely manageable as a new energy surged through my body. I felt remarkably alive. *What's been outlined here tonight would certainly be one hell of a life*, I pondered.

'I appreciate we have covered some really big topics here tonight,' said The Oracle, 'so I hope I did them justice.'

More hands went up immediately, eager to explore further. But that was not to be.

Part Four

THE END

'Before I answer another question,' proclaimed The Oracle, 'I should point out that it's late, and many of you will need to get home in readiness for tomorrow.'

He was right. I looked at my watch expecting it to be nearing 9pm and was taken aback when I realized it had just passed midnight. The time had simply evaporated.

'Your questions have been invaluable,' he said, 'and I feel confident that you will leave here ready to tackle life head on. I also feel my opening promise is intact. That is, you will leave here knowing *how to live* your life.

'Although we have covered a lot of territory, I hope a clear formula has also emerged which is captured simply in our Life Plan.' He was pointing at the drawing on the whiteboard once again ...

Step 1: I have committed to a divine and audacious intention
I am here to realize my full potential and help all those I come into contact with realize theirs. I will do this by: Loving and being loved. Doing my Great Work. Maintaining a healthy body and mind and reconnecting to the spirit. Securing my financial freedom. Enjoying the journey.

Step 2:
I have embraced
a new set of
limitless beliefs
The 12 Core Beliefs

Step 3:
I act in alignment
with my virtuous
Code of Conduct
The A to Z of Life

Step 4: I rest knowing what I seek is already mine

Step 5: I have immersed myself in the seven great love affairs

Step 6: I am doing my Great Work

Step 7: I practice the 10 steps of perfect health and transcendence

Step 8: I have secured my financial freedom by implementing the seven laws

Step 9: I stay on track, leverage myself and enjoy the journey

'And your day will look something like this in order to make it a reality,' said The Oracle, pointing to his daily routine diagram.

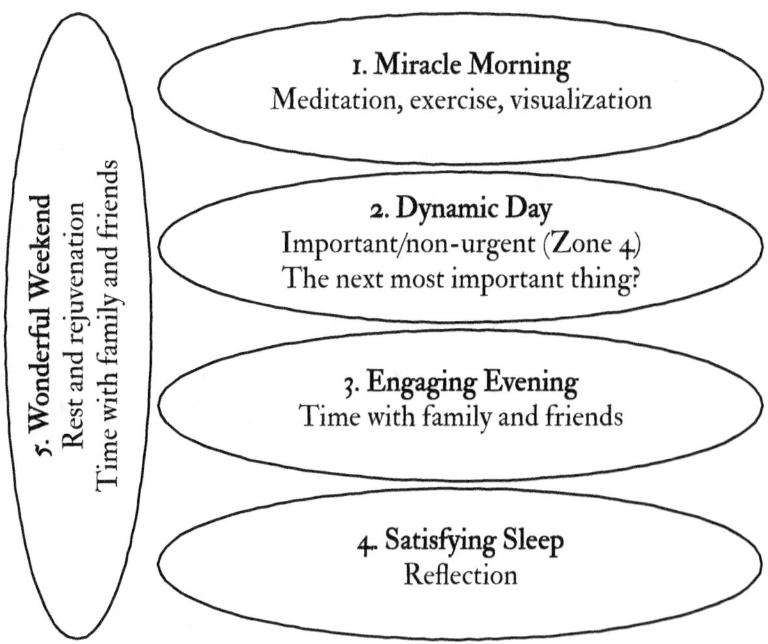

'This, my friends, is your roadmap for success and lasting happiness. This is the path to a future both spectacular and breathtaking. Your life's work.'

He paused, and I relished the opportunity to sit with this thought for a moment longer, for this was indeed an important moment. After all, how often does someone give you the answer everyone seems to be looking for, but no one seems to know? *How should we live our life?* I felt I now contained within my hands life's key.

The Oracle reached for the glass of water near him and took a sip before continuing.

'And please don't waste time focusing on those things you cannot control. As I meet people around the world, I am often presented with three scenarios about the future. There's a group that believe we are on the cusp of a new and enlightened era of humanity. A golden age of enlightenment. At the other end of the spectrum, there's a group that believe we are at the point of self-destruction, of extinction. Then there's the third group that seem to believe things will stay largely as they are.

'The reality, however, is that the life you end up living, whether that be an ordinary life or a remarkable life, will have very little to do with what's happening in the world at large. That's just a distraction, background noise, a smoke screen.

'What will have the greatest impact on your life is *not* the external environment that you walk into when you leave this room here tonight, but your internal environment. What you do at a personal level. The changes you make to yourself, your beliefs and behaviors, and the actions you take will determine the quality of your life.

'The biggest challenge you are likely to face is your own fear, self-doubt and anxiety. Your own self-talk. Yet there is no need to be fearful and full of doubt. You can relax, do your best and enjoy the journey knowing that your best will be good enough.

'In that sense, you are in control far more than most people are willing to admit. You can prepare for what might happen and you can respond appropriately to what does happen. The *Ninefold Path* gives you what you require in that regard. Beyond that there is little you can do, so follow the system and enjoy the journey.

'You don't need to be perfect either,' he added for support. 'I am certainly not perfect. But that's okay. I know what I need to do and, like you, my life is simply a work in progress. I may be a little further along the road than some of you, but it's not where you start that counts.

'"There are three classes of people," said the great Leonardo Da Vinci: "those who see; those who see when they are shown; and those who do not see." Maybe you are already one of the lucky few who see? Who knows, but you can now all consider yourself *shown*. So, take that knowledge and get out there and put it into action.

'Before you go however,' The Oracle lowered his voice to a whisper, 'I want you to listen carefully as I have one final, very important thing to tell you.'

At this we all leaned in expectantly, seeking that last treasure we could take away with as he begun in hushed tones ...

' ... Each morning as you lift your head off the pillow, remember you have everything you need.'

After a long silence, he executed a small bow and the evening was officially over. The room erupted into great applause.

As I got up to leave, I felt compelled to thank The Oracle for what he had helped me to see in the short time that we had spent together.

'That was truly fabulous,' I said, as I shuffled past him on the way to the exit. 'Thank you so much.'

'Good to see you again,' he said, turning toward me and placing a hand gently on my shoulder. 'Thank you for coming.'

'Well ... I'm so happy that I did. And surprised I must say. I wouldn't normally do a spur-of-the-moment thing like this. But I am looking forward to putting into action what I have learnt here tonight.'

'That's so gratifying to hear,' responded The Oracle with a warm smile. 'What is your name?'

'Chris,' I responded.

'Well, Chris,' he said, 'keep in mind what happened to the person that suddenly got everything they ever wanted.'

'What's that?'

'They lived happily ever after,' he said, breaking into a broad smirk that lit up his face from ear to ear.

And so, that's what I did ...

I lived happily ever after.

.... with a little bit of help putting this into action.

But that's another story.

WHAT NEXT?

I hope you have enjoyed *The Oracle*, and I trust it has helped you understand what you need to do to live a remarkable life!

Now you are underway, now you have embarked on the hero's journey, I would suggest you keep going. If you are ready to fly solo, then simply take the information from this book and begin to apply it in your life. If you are looking for some further guidance, then I have a few options available to assist you further:

- **Masterclass:** *The Oracle* does a great job outlining *what* you need to do and *why*! If you need further assistance in understanding *how* to do it, then we have a Masterclass available for that purpose. This simple but highly effective online course is designed to guide you through a process that will incorporate and embed the philosophy outlined here into your daily life.

- **Workshops:** If you would prefer some in-person interaction, guidance and assistance to incorporate and embed this philosophy into your daily life then we have a series of regular one-day workshop throughout the year that you can attend. You will leave these workshops with a new *Personal Life Plan* and *Daily Routine* in hand, ready to go out there and make your new life a reality.

- **Coaching:** If you are seriously committed to living a remarkable life and you want to accelerate the process then you may consider my one-on-one coaching program. This 11-month program is designed as the ultimate transformative process. Here we will explore the depths of your soul together and understand what it is that currently makes you tick – so you truly know yourself – before I personally guide you through the *Ninefold Path* and help you to embed it into your daily life. Here you get to spend 11 months of your life like most people won't, so you can spend the rest of your life living like most people really, really want to – but can't. But be warned, the process is truly transformative and life changing, so it's not for the faint hearted.

I continually find that the single most important difference between those who go on to live a *remarkable* life and those who live an *ordinary* life is that those who live a remarkable life seek out a guide – to point out the subtle changes that will make all the difference. So please use the above resources to act as your guide. I am here to help, and I am confident I can help you to live a remarkable as opposed to ordinary life. But you will need to get moving, or it will be too late!

You can find further information regarding the above at:

www.lachlancameron.com

Appendix A

THE NINE RULES
OF PARENTING

Rule #1 Firm love: You need to provide soft hands that do not move. Lots of vitamin N. That is, don't hesitate to say 'no' on a regular basis, and expect your children to obey.

Rule #2 Contribution: Expect your children to make a significant and meaningful contribution to the running of the household. Ensure they do this via their own list of allocated tasks that are age appropriate, evolving with time.

Rule #3 Unconditional love: Love who they are no matter what. Do not expect them to be perfect but help them to be whole.

Rule #4 Simplicity: Provide few toys and allow little screen time. Allow them to be bored and then watch the creativity flow.

Rule #5 Quantity, quality and teaching: Spend large amounts of quality time together. In that time, use every opportunity you can to teach them all you possibly can about the world. Best of all this can occur by simply involving them in what you do. You don't need to create a separate 'child' orientated world.

Rule #6 High expectations and failure: Have high expectations of them but expect them to fail regularly along the way. When they do fail, don't make it such a big thing that they feel they need to be perfect or hide their failures from you.

Rule #7 Empowerment: Let them make their own decisions and solve their own problems. Don't be a 'snowplow' parent, forging a path for them. It does them no favors. Besides, it's okay for them to fail in a safe environment. They are hardwired for struggle, so they will survive. Provide responsibility if they can demonstrate their ability to handle it but take it away when they fail to hold up their end of the bargain.

Rule #8 Be influenced: Allow yourself to be genuinely influenced and changed by your children. Don't just open yourself up to what they have to teach you but expect them to teach you more than you can teach them. Your life should be profoundly changed by the insights they expose you to, and, in turn, they will be much more open to your influence on them. This is of course because the best way to influence someone is to be influenced by them.

Rule #9 Focus on strengths: Finally, focus on your children's strengths rather than always trying to correct their weaknesses. Recognize that parents suffer from a negativity bias, thanks to evolutionary development, and are therefore prone to focus on weaknesses. You will need to overcompensate to get this right.

Appendix B

A NEW WORLD VIEW

You see life as a wonderful adventure, full of hope and possibility, with no need for fear and doubt. For the real you cannot be afraid, it cannot be frightened.

You work harmoniously in collaboration with the spirit, that unseen source or intelligent form, that permeates and fills the interspaces of the universe. That unmanifested energy out of which all things emerge.

You recognize that this is an intelligence far greater than us, there to bring forth what is inside us. Something it desperately wants and needs to do, for ultimately it must work through us to get things done. You appreciate that life works better, has more meaning and is eminently more joyous and easier when you reconnect, co-create and live in collaboration with this unseen spirit.

You know that there is no need to worship another. You are simply seeking to be in vibratory accord with your divine self, your true self – the spirit – and the closer you move to be in alignment with your true self the greater your genius. You are your own healer, hero and leader. If you have to worship anything, you worship nature.

You know that the whole of life is one, the seen and the unseen, matter and spirit. The universe is an unbroken, unified whole despite the illusion of being a multitude of separate objects.

You appreciate that the world changes when we perceive it differently. Those things that take on the appearance and feel of form are just vibrating energy. The true nature of the world is not solidity, stability, and permanence but perpetual motion. As a consequence, you no longer grasp or cling to that which is transitory. The material is never coveted or overly relied upon because you recognize that the most important things in life are invisible. Nevertheless, you see the physical abundance that surrounds you as something to be appreciated and enjoyed.

You know that life will continually go up and down. It is both predictable and unpredictable. We get both what we want and don't want. You therefore relax into change and see the world afresh. You flourish on both the good days and the bad days. You appreciate the world as it is, not as you would like it to be. You realize we have limited control over how the cards of life are dealt, but you do control the hand you play once they are dealt. As for the people and situations we typically find most difficult, you recognize that they are the best teachers in life.

You see love as the divine power. So, you approach all you do with a simple but powerful question: how would love respond? If I loved myself, how would I respond? If I loved you, how would I respond? If I loved what I was doing, how would I respond? And you respond accordingly, knowing that it's never loving that hurts, it's not loving.

You seek to get to the essence or true nature of things and people. You look for the truth behind appearance, lift the veil of misperception. You understand that in quietness all things are answered. So, you use this technique to escape the limits of normal perception and see things as if for the first time, to think beyond the confines of culture.

You appreciate that the only time you ever have is this moment and that you are born anew in every moment. You have already had a thousand deaths and a thousand births in this lifetime alone, so you leave your past and become your present now, a new person now. And now. And now. And now. And now.

You realise that you are a manifestation of the spirit in material form. A divine being having a human experience. That your essential nature is pure immortal energy. That you are in this world but not of it.

You realise that you are not separate from your source. It doesn't require work to become who you are. You simply need to get out of the way and allow yourself to unfold and to bloom as a flower might. You appreciate it's not about doing things a little better, it's about reclaiming your true identity, your true nature far beyond what's been claimed thus far. You are not some small, insignificant and powerless speck within the universe. Quite the contrary – you are the universe, and the universe is within you. That makes you all powerful and limitless. You are therefore no better than anyone or anything else and no one else is better than you, but you are capable of manifesting anything you choose with your intention and attention. You are a vehicle for divine expression, and you can realize that potential by taking action in the physical world. Paradoxically, it is through losing the small self, the false self, and aligning to your true self that your greatest personal power is gained. Far from losing control, this brings to life all your dormant potentialities.

You appreciate that although the world doesn't belong to humans, it does need humans to belong to it. You therefore engage and make your contribution. You bring forth your precious present, you bring forth what is within you, by following the *Ninefold Path*. You therefore ...

1. Commit to a divine and audacious intention.

2. Embrace a new set of limitless beliefs.

3. Act in alignment with your virtuous Code of Conduct.

4. Rest knowing what you seek is already yours.

5. Immerse yourself in the seven great love affairs.

6. Do your Great Work.

7. Practice the 10 steps of perfect health and transcendence.

8. Secure your financial freedom by implementing the seven laws, and ...

9. Stay on track, leverage yourself, and enjoy the journey.

No more, no less.

You do not fear death, you let it in. You see it as nothing more than the movement of the spirit from one domain to another. Like a wave in the ocean, death is simply a return to the ocean of energy from whence you came. From which another wave will be formed and then another and another. Death's presence therefore brings a welcome and necessary urgency to your life. It reminds you to live each day as though it could be your last even though you continue to plan as though you will live forever. You realise death's great gift is to motivate you to live a life with no regrets, forcing you to seize the day and ensure you do not miss the opportunity to be fabulous. You therefore see death as the best invention of life. A reminder that you have nothing to lose in getting out there and living life to the fullest.

ACKNOWLEDGMENTS

Thanks to ...

Firstly, I am incredibly grateful to those that acted as my guide in life during those early formulative years. My mother and father, my grandfather John Teague, Rob and Virginia Jones, Joe and Jutta Schall, Andrew McQueen, Johnny Palfreyman, Julian and Edwina Doyle, Sally and Sheldon Cohen, Brian Randall, Ron Walker, coach David Boykett and neighbour Peter Macaulay. Thank you for all you did and the guidance you provided.

Thank you to the wonderful crew at Linderman Island who kicked off this journey. I am also incredibly grateful to those that facilitated some truly transformative experiences during my working life. Ed Vance, Chris Nash, Jim Hamblen, Don Bartlett, Bob Montgomery, George Herscu, Neil Bryson, Steve McMillan, Neville Harpham, Susan MacDonald, Richard Clark, Stuart Hornery, Peter McMillan, Robert Johnson, Peter Joseph, Nic Lyons, Michael O'Brien, Neil Tobin, Anthony McNulty, Mark Fookes, Jol and Rachael Keeble.

A special thank you to my wife Bronwyn, and children Matilda and Jack, who have been such an inspiration and co-conspirators through this journey we call life.

To Sarah Wood, Sonya Richards, Andrew Richards, Harry Bell, David Coggin, Stuart MacLeod-Smith, Cameron Price, Geoffrey Bowell, Martin Karaffa, Hugh Batters, Julian Josem and Andrew Griffiths, my thanks go to you for your review and feedback on various aspects or early drafts of this book, which contributed greatly to the final result.

I am grateful to Warren Buffett, whose generosity and wisdom have taught us all so much on the art of investing.

I am grateful to Joseph Campbell for his groundbreaking work and explanation of the hero's journey.

I am grateful to Michael Singer, author of *The Untethered Soul*, for his teaching on surrender and remaining open.

It was Dr Seuss, surely the greatest philosopher of modern times, who said: 'Be who you are and say what you feel, because those who mind don't matter and those who matter don't mind.'

It was David Foster Wallace, in his excellent book *This is Water*, who tells the story of the two young fish swimming along as they happen to meet an older fish swimming the other way.

It was Wallace D. Wattles in his wonderful book, *The Science of Getting Rich*, who first introduced me to the empowering notion that: 'There is a thinking stuff from which all things are made, and which, in its original state, permeates, penetrates, and fills the interspaces of the universe. A thought in this substance produces the thing that is imagined by the thought. A person can form things in his thought, and, by impressing his thought upon formless substance, can cause the thing he thinks about to be created.'

I am forever grateful to Richard Koch for sharing his incredible insight around the 80/20 principle and the Star Principle. I would highly recommend all of his work to you.

It was Ralph Waldo Emerson who said: 'The only person you are destined to become is the person you decide to be; and this time, like all times, is a very good one, if we know what to do with it.'

It was Dr Pippa Grange who said: 'Losing does not turn me into a loser. We are not worth less if we fail. Losing is for winners.'

It was Tim Johnson who explained to me that it doesn't matter what speed you are progressing in life, as long as there is some forward momentum.

It was the incredibly insightful Yung Pueblo who proposed: 'You are your own healer, hero and leader.' And suggested you cannot reach out to others for the love that you are not giving yourself. He also reminded us that when you heal yourself you heal the world.

It was Benjamin Franklin who said: 'The things that hurt, instruct', and warned us about the risk of becoming 'old too soon and wise too late'.

It was Viktor Frankl who said: 'Between stimulus and response there is a space. In that space is our power to choose our response. In our response lies our growth and our freedom.'

It was Stephen Covey who brought to our attention the importance of focusing on your circle of influence and the need to begin with the end in mind.

It was Anita Roddick who said, 'If you ever think you're too small to have an impact, I want you to remember what it's like going to bed with a mosquito in the room.'

It was Steve Jobs that pointed out to us that those crazy enough to think they can change the world are the ones that do.

It was Mahatma Gandhi who taught us to be the change we seek.

It was Ernest Hemingway who said: 'There is nothing noble in being superior to your fellow man; true nobility is being superior to your former self.'

It was Denis Waitley who first pointed out to me that the reason most people never reach their goals is that they don't define them in the first place.

It was W. Clement Stone who said, 'there is little difference in people, but that little difference makes a big difference.'

It was Carl Jung who first explained to us the 'shadow' as a symbol that represents the hidden side of every human psyche.

Thank you to Malcolm Gladwell who pointed out in his informative and captivating book *David and Goliath* that contrary to popular understanding David will typically defeat Goliath, assuming he accepts his weaknesses and chooses an unconventional strategy that plays to his unique strength.

It was Edith Eger who, in her astonishing book *The Choice*, said: 'Cooperation is the name of the game; to transcend your own needs and commit yourself to someone or something outside yourself.'

It was Elbert Hubbard who said, 'people who never do any more than they get paid for will never get paid for any more than they do'.

It was Robert K Greenleaf who said, 'there is very little sustained performance at the level of excellence – of any kind, anywhere – without continuous coaching'.

It was Bruce Lipton, in his wonderful book *The Honeymoon Effect*, who first introduced me to the concept of constructive interference in relationships.

It was Rolf Potts who first brought to the attention of the world the benefits of being a vagabond.

It was the incredibly wise and inspiring Hal Elrod that coined the term *Miracle Morning* in his book of the same name, one I encourage you all to read.

It was the genius of Roald Dahl through the remarkable Willy Wonka who challenged Charlie not to forget what happened to the man who suddenly got everything he always wanted.

It was the inspirational movie *E-Motion* that brought to my attention the idea that from the moment you lift your head off the pillow, you have everything you need.

It was Ryan Holiday who coined the term *The Obstacle Is The Way*, in his excellent book of the same name.

Thank you to Leo Price and Ben Symons, for starting the debate on competition that historic night in Henley and whether you can in fact have a win/win situation in life.

Thank you to Guy Lawrence for his truly illuminating podcast that I look forward to each week.

Thank you to Eckhart Tolle who has done so much to bring to our attention the Power of Now.

Thank you to Deepak Chopra, Paulo Coelho and don Miguel Ruiz who have done so much to bring the importance of spirituality to the attention of the western world. Your books and teachings are truly inspirational.

Thank you to Ben Hourigan for your early assistance with this book, and to Claire McGregor for your initial editing advice which was incredibly helpful.

Many thanks must also go to Michael Hanrahan and the team at Publish Central who helped me finally make this all a reality.

Finally, a very special thank you to Angus Parnham. Not only for your proofreading and feedback on early drafts of this book but more importantly your various thoughts and additions: introducing me to Jamie Anderson's thoughts on grief. Adding the important third step in releasing trapped emotions. The inclusion of 'Vagabonding' as a key step in securing your freedom. The inclusion of 'Rest and Re-energize' as a key step in obtaining perfect health. Your reflections on what made your brother Ned's life such a remarkable one. The question around fear as a motivator. The importance of empathy. The importance of self-talk. Your contribution to the discussion on addiction. Bringing greater personality to The Oracle and vulnerability to Chris. All contributions that significantly improved the final text.

None of this would have been possible without all of your input and support.

www.ingramcontent.com/pod-product-compliance
Lightning Source LLC
Chambersburg PA
CBHW051107050726
47592CB00002B/703